Once an essential part of every eighteenth-century gentleman's education, carving is today a professional skill largely practised by amateurs — sometimes with disastrous results.

Expert Paul Southey, himself a dab hand with a sharp blade, believes that a knowledge of the fundamental elements is the key to learning to carve quickly, easily and well.

Both professional cooks and reluctant carvers persuaded to do a hacksaw job on the weekend joint will find Paul Southey's advice, backed by over 150 step-by-step illustrations, invaluable and easy to follow. *The Expert Carver* earns its place in every well-equipped kitchen, so that whether you are faced with a supermarket chicken, a crown roast, or the glories of a saddle of venison, you can wield the knife with complete confidence.

Paul Southey is a photographer, designer and brilliant cook. His interest in cooking was first aroused by the enormous variety of food and cuisines available in his native country, South Africa. In 1980 his book *Gourmet Cooking without Meat* laid the foundation for a new trend in vegetarian cookery and was among the Top Twenty Books of the Year of the United States Taste Makers Award. He is not a vegetarian but became interested in the challenge of recipe and menu planning using vegetable and dairy products to suit Western taste.

Apart from cooking and entertaining, Paul Southey's other interests include wine, gardening, music, mathematics and information technology.

The Expert Carver

HOW TO CARVE
MEAT, POULTRY AND GAME

PAUL SOUTHEY

CENTURY

LONDON · MELBOURNE · AUCKLAND · JOHANNESBURG

Illustrations © Century Hutchinson 1987

First published in 1987 by
Century Hutchinson Ltd, Brookmount House, 62–65 Chandos Place,
Covent Garden, London WC2N 4NW

Century Hutchinson Australia Pty Ltd,
PO Box 496, 16–22 Church Street, Hawthorn, Victoria 3122 Australia

Century Hutchinson New Zealand Ltd,
PO Box 40–086, Glenfield, Auckland 10, New Zealand

Century Hutchinson South Africa Pty Ltd,
PO Box 337, Bergvlei, 2012 South Africa

Photoset by Deltatype, Ellesmere Port in 10½ pt Linotron Sabon.
Designed by Gwyn Lewis
Illustrations by Rob Shone

Printed and bound in Great Britain by Mackays, Chatham, Kent

Southey, Paul
    The expert carver.
    1. Carving (Meat, etc.)——Amateur's manuals
    I. Title
    642'.6   TX885

ISBN 0–7126–1766–3

Contents

Introduction

In earlier times carving was the prerogative of high officials in royal or princely households and it was considered an essential part of a gentleperson's education. Legend has it that Louis Philippe enjoyed demonstrating his skill at carving joints, poultry and game and delighted his guests by doing so at special banquets.

You, as the cook, are in a very good position to have a preview of the action because you can spy out the land, as it were, by examining the meat or bird before it is cooked. By moving the relative parts you can distinguish the position of the joints and the thickness of the flesh, which will provide reliable guidelines for carving when the cooking is done.

Mrs Beeton tells of a gourmand who, reminiscing about the proprietor of the Savoy restaurant in London, at the turn of the century, claimed that, 'he made of his carving such a performance that the orchestra stopped dead and, taking his stand at the head of the room, M. Joseph cut slices, one after another, with vigorous single cuts, holding the bird, meanwhile, on a fork in his left hand. As I watched him, calmly and solemnly, cutting a duck into neat pieces with a long, thin knife, I was reminded, in an irreverent moment, of the Chinese torture of the Ling Ching, in which the executioner slashes at his victim without hitting a vital part, in fifty cuts.'

I do not suggest that you should emulate such virtuosity; it might distract your friends and prevent them from enjoying the products of your labour. But following the philosophy of moderation in all things *The Expert Carver* explains the fundamental elements of carving. Presenting a blow by blow account or, should I say, precise cut followed by precise cut, it explains with notes and illustrations how to carve easily, quickly and well. There is no point in perfecting a technique that would stand a successful surgeon in good stead if the food is cold before your guests have a chance to sample it.

The Expert Carver includes a section on the equipment you will need for the preparation of the meat before carving and the various items which make the actual process of carving easier. Having had the embarrassing experience of attempting to carve badly prepared meat, I also tell you how to make things easier for yourself before you start cooking.

I wish you bon appetit.

Equipment

Knives

Good carving, butchery and fish preparation depend on sharp knives. I consider good-quality stainless steel is quite adequate for general kitchen use, although it requires a little more effort when sharpening and it certainly does not take as keen an edge as genuine carbon steel. Some cooks prefer a blade of carbon steel because it takes a much finer edge than stainless steel when it is sharpened. But carbon steel knives do have their disadvantages; they rust and should not be used for cutting fruit or tomatoes. Plastic handles or composition are preferable to wooden ones as they can be immersed in water when washing up and some even resist the attentions of dishwashers.

If you are investing in a new set of knives it is advisable to examine the products of various manufacturers and check with any relevant consumer associations' reports. Remember that the balance of the knife and the comfort of the handle are almost as important as the flexibility and the sharpness of the blade. When you have decided on a manufacturer, buy one knife and use it for a couple of weeks, before buying the complete set. This will enable you to assess whether it suits you, is easy to sharpen and keeps its edge when you have sharpened it.

Knives are a personal matter with cooks, so I, not necessarily following conventional methods and techniques, have my own favourites. Most of the time I use only four different knives for all meat and fish preparation:

9

- a 10 cm (4 in) fine-pointed, straight-backed, wedge-shaped knife for most boning of meat and fish
- I change to a 20 cm (8 in) fine-pointed, straight-backed, wedge-shaped knife when preparing a larger joint such as a sirloin of beef or a whole loin of pork
- an odd and, I believe, irreplaceable 20 cm (8 in) radial-pointed, flat, flexible, curved-blade knife for boning a shoulder of lamb or veal, or a hand and spring of pork, as the blade follows the line of the bone
- a curved, radial-pointed, wedge-shaped knife with a blade some 30 cm (12 in) long for filleting flat fish such as sole or plaice; I also use this knife for preparing meat for casseroles, pies and stews.

But there are many other knives as well as these you might prefer to use. Here is the full range:

Straight-backed, fine-pointed, wedge-shaped knives

These are general purpose kitchen knives used for chopping, cutting, paring and slicing. They come in a range of sizes from about 10 cm (4 in) to 30 cm (12 in).

For meat and fish preparation a knife of this type with a firm, short blade of some 10 cm (4 in) with a good point is useful for separating and cutting the tendons around a ball and socket joint when boning a leg of lamb or shoulder of mutton and when dissecting the spine, rib cage and fin framework out of a round fish. It is essential when boning poultry as a larger knife is too unwieldy. A larger version of about 20 cm (8 in) is useful when preparing or boning larger joints of meat. An even larger one with a 25 cm (10 in) blade might be useful if you are dealing with large cuts of meat frequently; it is also useful for cutting even strips or slabs of pork fat when larding or barding lean meat or game.

Curved, radial-pointed, wedge-shaped blades

These are used for boning, carving, filleting and slicing. They used to come in a range of sizes from about 15 cm (6 in) to 30 cm (12 in) but they have become increasingly difficult to find in any other than a couple of larger sizes. They are worth the search as they are the ideal knife for filleting fish and boning and preparing larger joints of meat.

Use a knife with a long blade, about 30 cm (12 in) long, for filleting flat fish such as sole or plaice. A wide blade helps to keep the cutting edge parallel to the spine and the bones. This knife is also ideal for slicing large sausages and terrines if they do not contain too much fat; otherwise a serrated knife will be required.

Carving knives

Professional cooks use knives up to 40 cm (16 in) for carving; however, for normal home use, in the dining room or the kitchen, a blade 23 cm (10 in) long is quite adequate.

Serrated knives

Serrated knives are used for carving ham or smoked salmon, as the hollows between the serrations prevent the fat from clogging the cutting edge and dragging the meat.

But serrated does not mean saw-edged. The serrations should be just a little less than 1 cm (⅜ in) wide. The almost standard measurement is 30 cm (12 in) long. Ensure that the knife and blade are well balanced or you will have difficulty in controlling the blade when you are carving and will land up with uneven and wavering slices.

Saw-edged knives

Various manufacturers have produced sets of kitchen knives which have very fine indentations along the cutting edge. I have found that the smaller ones are good for slicing tomatoes and

11

vegetables thinly if they are kept really sharp. The larger knives cut very efficiently but, and this is an entirely personal view, I find that they put my teeth on edge if I use them for cutting meat as there is a slight jarring sensation as they cut through the fibres of the meat. Sharpen them on a steel as you would any other knife.

Ever-sharp knives

Using recent discoveries resulting from space research, some manufacturers are producing knives with particularly hard steel claiming that they will not require frequent sharpening, if at all. While this is obviously possible one suspects that, when the time comes to resharpen them, the steel from which they were made will be equally resistant to one's efforts at sharpening them. However, if you are like me, you will probably have lost the knife before it needs sharpening.

Electric carving knives

I suppose I should mention electric carving knives here. As the saying goes, some of my best friends use them, but I have always considered them silly gadgets only useful to the physically handicapped or to people possessing an abysmal lack of confidence and skill in sharpening and using good knives. Many handicapped people, however, have complained that they would be very much more useful if they could be made lighter. I admit, speaking from hard experience, that they can be useful when cutting through pork crackling which has not been adequately prepared before roasting and I, incognito, have found them very helpful when carving sucking pig or very large sirloins. If you are going to invest in one, ensure that the blades have a safe, quick-release mechanism, that there is a pilot light to show when the power is switched on and that the blades can be sharpened easily.

Remember to issue your guests with protective clothing so that they will not be hit by the pieces of flying meat when you become overexcited by the unexpected speed and efficiency of the gadget. Don't use the knife to emphasize a conversational gambit or you might remove the colonel's whiskers.

Oyster knives, clam openers and claw crackers

While oyster knives, clam openers and claw crackers are not knives in the strict sense of the word they fall more easily into this section so I shall discuss them here.

The oyster knife should have a strong, rigid blade of a little less than 5 cm (2 in) and a handle which fits comfortably into the hand. Clam openers work on the shearing principle and at least guarantee that you do not stab your hand instead of the clam. Make sure that they are strongly constructed and are easily sharpened. Claw crackers are used for breaking lobster and crab claws and are a little more controlled in their operation than a hammer or kitchen cleaver.

Storage and sharpening

Good-quality, sharp knives are essential to the whole concept and practice of carving; but they must be kept in perfect condition. Store them in separate slots so that there is no chance of one blade notching another or points getting bent or broken. I recommend wooden or plastic slots as I have found that knives are inclined to drop off magnetic bars and inevitably get damaged.

There is a calm satisfaction in using a traditional steel to sharpen knives and its convenience allows it to be used mid-session to improve the edge of the knife to tackle a tricky bit of carving. To be really efficient, a steel should be 30 cm (12 in) long and well hardened with a good, but not too abrasive, surface.

Study the illustrations and instructions below and master the technique of using a steel to sharpen your knives; you will be astounded at the difference it will make to even simple cutting operations in your cooking. Get into the habit of always sharpening a knife before using it.

The following instructions are based on right-handed orientation; if you are left-handed you will need to reverse the positions. Hold the steel in the left hand and the knife in your right hand with the sharp side of the blade pointing towards you. Stroke the blade of the knife from the handle to the point across the steel,

1   10 cm (4 in) fine-pointed, wedge-shaped, straight-backed knife
2   20 cm (8 in) fine-pointed, wedge-shaped, straight-backed knife
3   20 cm (8 in) radial-pointed, curved blade knife
4   30 cm (12 in) radial-pointed, curved blade knife
5   25 cm (10 in) carving knife
6   30 cm (12 in) serrated knife
7   Steel
8   Cleaver
9   Saw-edged knife
10   Kitchen saw
11   Electric carving knife
12   Claw crackers
13   Poultry shears
14   5 cm (2 in) oyster knife
15   Carving fork
16   Spatula
17   Scissor-action tongs
18   Pin
19   Skewers
20   Larding needles
21   Carving board

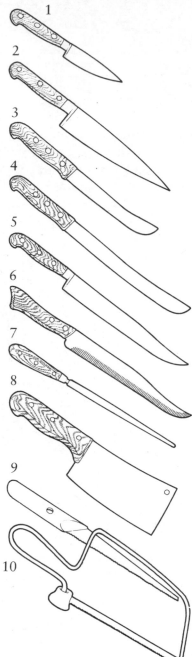

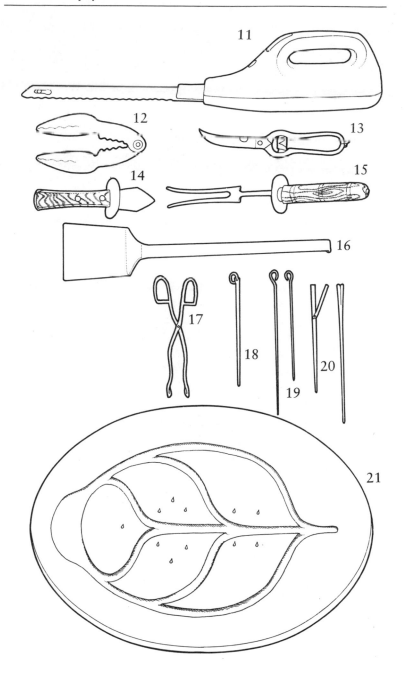

sliding the blade away from you while maintaining an angle of approximately 45° between the blade and the steel. (See illustrations below and note the position of the knife at the end of the movement.)

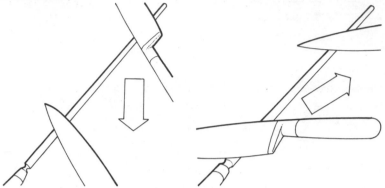

This double action speeds up the process. Repeat it ten or fifteen times. Now turn the blade over so that the sharp edge is away from you and again stroke the blade of the knife from the handle to the point across the steel but this time sliding the blade towards you. Don't worry – the sharp side of the blade is away from you. Repeat this ten or fifteen times. The sheikhs of Araby tested the keenness of their swords by throwing a silk scarf into the air and slicing it in half as it floated. I suggest, instead, that you test the keenness of your knife by cutting a tomato into thin slices, ensuring that the whole of the blade, from the absolute point to the handle, has a really fine cutting edge.

If you are really unable to master the technique then invest in an electric knife sharpener and follow the manufacturer's instructions.

Slicing machines

If you serve a lot of cold rolled meat, charcuterie and continental sausages, you might find it worth investing in an electric slicing machine. Follow the manufacturer's instructions, press the switch, and 'hey presto', you should have a pile of neat, identical slices waiting to be arranged on a plate. That is, if you have remembered to put the meat in the machine in the first place . . .

Poultry shears

The purists will complain that kitchen or poultry shears are not part of the legitimate battery of carving equipment. But there is no doubt they have their uses; their main snag is that they can splinter the bones and leave sharp pieces in the meat. But with care and by keeping the blades really sharp, they can make life much easier, when removing the drumsticks and thighs from a chicken or cutting a smaller bird in half. You can see how to use them in the illustrations for dividing a small bird on page (74).

Forks

Forks come in two forms, the traditional with curved prongs and the cook's type with almost parallel prongs. I do not think that there is much to choose between the two. The essential facts are that the prongs should be sharp, about 2.5 cm (1 in) apart and about 8 cm (3 in) long.

There should be a very adequate guard, either in the form of a raised ledge around the handle or a sprig at right angles to the handle to prevent the carver getting cut if the knife slips.

Carving boards and platters

Having solved the equipment required for the actual cutting and carving of the meat, the time has come to discuss how to restrain it and prevent it from escaping its destiny. And also where we can dispose of the fruits of our labours in an efficient and decorative manner before passing them on to our expectant guests.

You can choose from platters made of wood, stainless steel, pewter or plate, china, pottery or oven-proof glass. Putting aesthetics to one side, my choice is between wood or metal. With these materials it is possible to incorporate a system of spikes which ensures that the dish and joint, or piece of meat, stay together and there is no chance of the meat suddenly sliding across the dish sending roast potatoes, garnish or trimmings flying across the table.

It is also an advantage if the platter or board has a system of channels leading to a hollow where the gravy or juices from the meat can accumulate to be spooned over each serving or added to the gravy boat if you wish.

Serving spatulas and scissor-action tongs

A wide serving spatula reduces the risk factor when handling a slice of carved meat, ballottine or even the more mundane meat loaf; similarly scissor-action tongs are excellent for serving rolls of crisp bacon or roast potatoes.

Pins, skewers and larding needles

A set of 9 cm (3½ in), 13 cm (5 in) and 18 cm (7 in) pins or skewers should enable you to carry out most procedures when preparing meat, poultry or fish. To see how to use them in meat preparation, see Improving on Nature (pages 106–108).

You will require three larding needles of some 20 cm (8 in), 25 cm (10 in) and 30 cm (12 in) to lard the leaner cuts of meat and game; the size of the larding needle dictates the thickness of the fat which can be inserted into the meat; if you are going to restrict yourself to only one, I suggest you choose 25 cm.

Kitchen saws and cleavers

Professional butchers use special saws to cut through bones, but unless you prepare a large quantity of meat you will find that a small DIY saw is perfectly adequate. See illustration (pages 14–15) and choose the one you prefer; whichever one you buy, ensure that the blade has fairly fine teeth. Note, however, that the bow variety limits the length of the cut that you are able to make, which might be inconvenient if you wish to cut along all the rib bones of a best end. I have found that the Chinese or Japanese cleavers are beautifully balanced and are effective in preparation of food from those countries. I prefer to use a saw for all bone cutting as a cleaver inevitably splinters the bone and one is then left with the task of removing the splinters.

Carving meat, poultry and game

There are certain axioms that should be part of meat carvers' lore to save them from the embarrassment of demonstrating that dilemma, beloved of oriental philosophers, of the meeting of an immovable object and an irresistible force. For immovable read uncarvable and for irresistible read the desperation of the would-be carver.

1 Only prime cuts should be roasted uncovered in the oven or barbecued over coals; pot roast or braise all others.

2 Rely on a good butcher or reliable supermarket to supply you with proper cuts of meat. Otherwise you may land up with anonymous, cobbled lumps which you will find impossible to carve successfully.

3 All meat should be brought to room temperature before it is placed in the oven, which should be preheated to the correct temperature. Remember that cooking time assessed by the weight of the joint is only a guide; it would be more accurate to calculate the time by volume and thickness, but for real accuracy a meat thermometer is essential. This enables you to keep a note of the preferred internal temperature for each type of meat and by experience you can learn to calculate the time required to produce the desired results.

4 Always allow the joint to 'rest' for 10–15 minutes after coming out of the oven, to allow the juices to spread throughout the joint again; they will have been forced to the extreme centre by the heat of the oven.

5 Sharpen the carving knife when you first place it on the table;

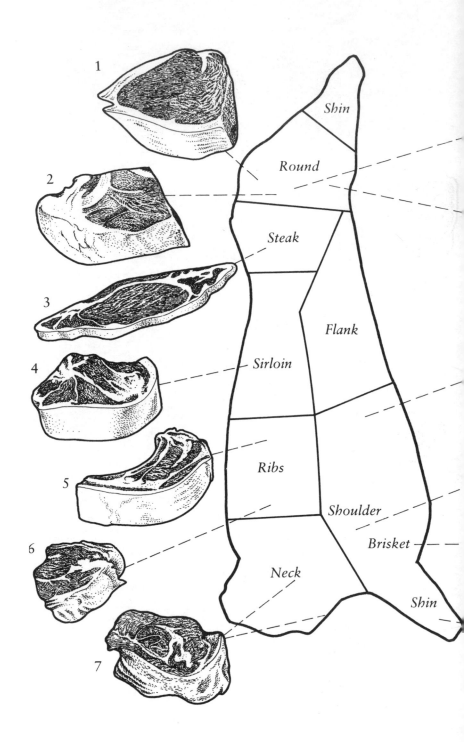

1

2

3

4

5

6

7

Shin

Round

Steak

Flank

Sirloin

Ribs

Shoulder

Brisket

Neck

Shin

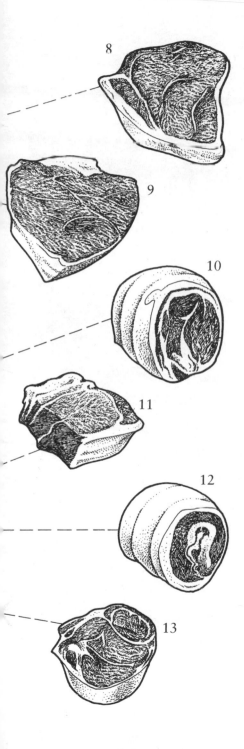

BEEF
The English Cuts

1   Silverside
2   Rump
3   Rump steak
4   Sirloin
5   Best rib
6   Chuck
7   Neck
8   Topside
9   Thick flank
10   Rolled ribs
11   Shoulder cut
12   Brisket
13   Shin

LAMB
The English Cuts

1 Shank end
2 Fillet of leg
3 Loin
4 Best end of neck
5 Middle of neck
6 Scrag end of neck
7 Leg
8 Chump chop
9 Loin chop
10 Breast
11 Cutlet
12 Shoulder

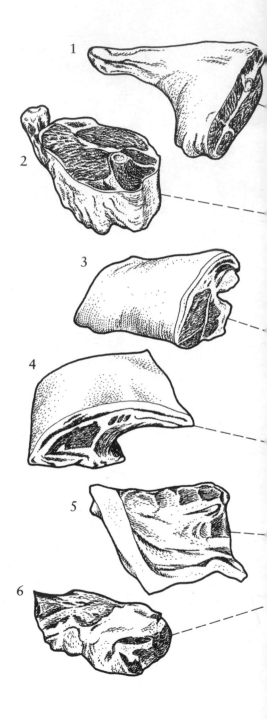

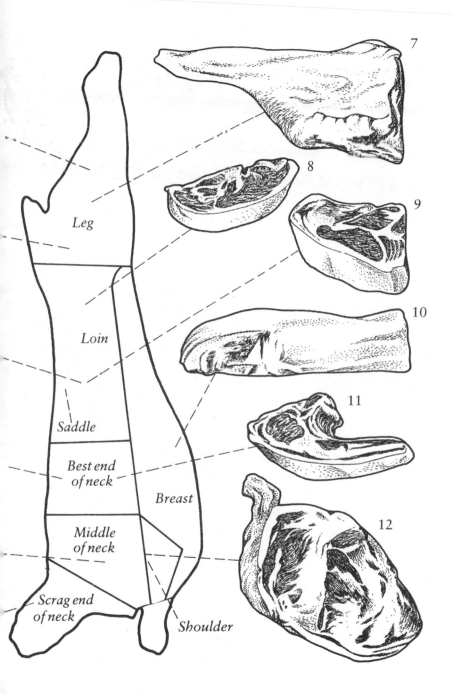

Leg

7

Loin

8

9

Saddle

10

Best end
of neck

11

Breast

Middle
of neck

12

Scrag end
of neck

Shoulder

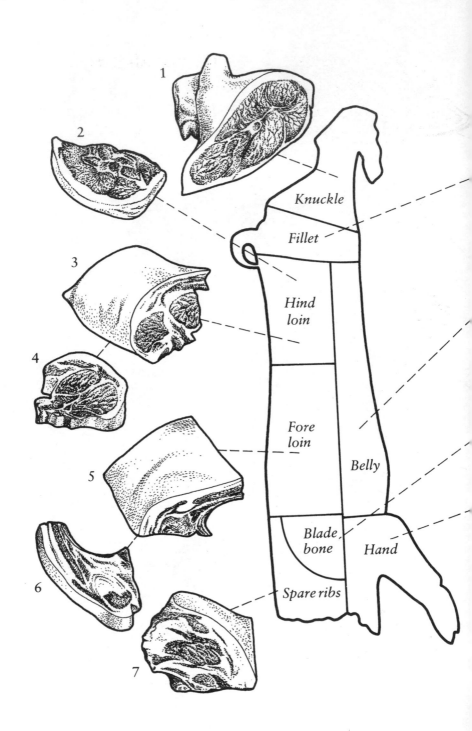

1

2

3

4

5

6

7

Knuckle

Fillet

Hind
loin

Fore
loin

Belly

Blade
bone

Hand

Spare ribs

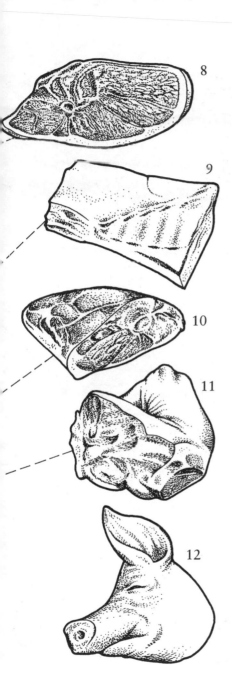

PORK

The English Cuts

1 Knuckle
2 Chump chop
3 Hind loin
4 Loin chop
5 Fore loin
6 Chop
7 Spare rib
8 Fillet
9 Belly
10 Blade bone
11 Hand
12 Head

VEAL
The English Cuts

1. Leg
2. Fillet steak
3. Loin
4. Best end of neck
5. Middle neck
6. Scrag end
7. Knuckle
8. Fillet end of leg
9. Breast
10. Half shoulder
11. Shoulder

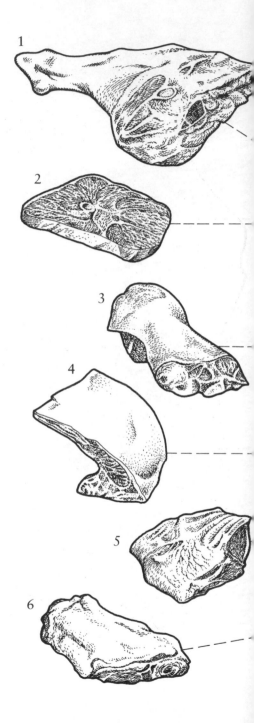

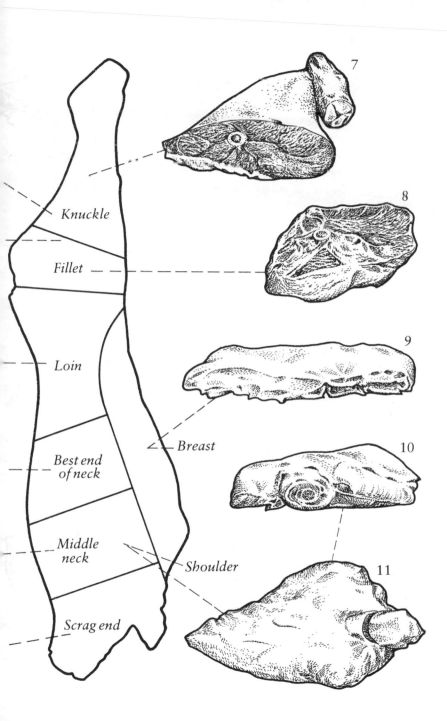

Knuckle

Fillet

Loin

Best end
of neck

Middle
neck

Shoulder

Scrag end

Breast

7

8

9

10

11

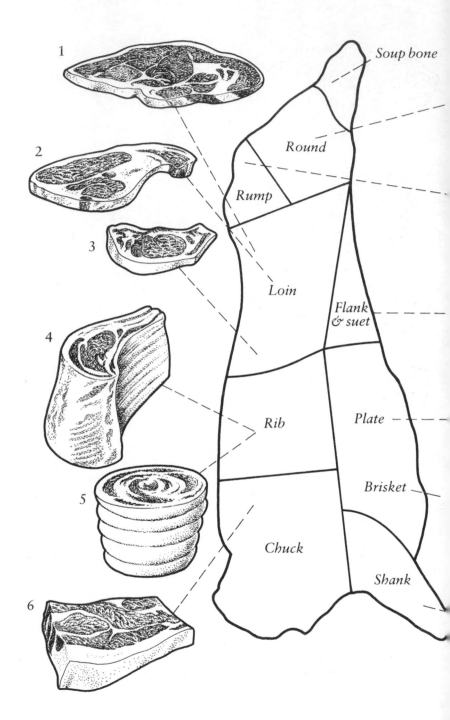

1

2

3

4

5

6

Soup bone

Round

Rump

Loin

Flank
& suet

Plate

Rib

Brisket

Chuck

Shank

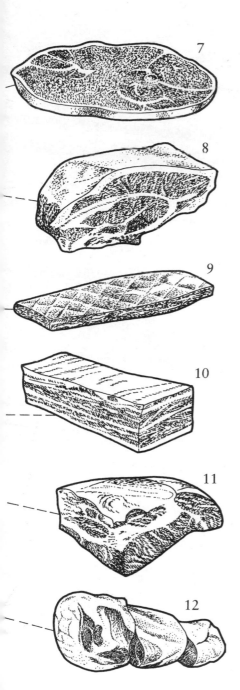

BEEF

The American Cuts

1 Sirloin steak
2 Porterhouse steak
3 Club steak
4 Standing rib roast
5 Rolled rib roast
6 Chuck roast
7 Round steak
8 Rump roast
9 Flank steak
10 Short ribs
11 Brisket (Corned beef)
12 Stew meat

LAMB
The American Cuts

1   Loin end of leg
2   American leg
3   English lamb chop
4   Loin chop
5   Rib chop
6   Crown roast
7   Neck slice
8   Leg steaks
9   'Frenched' leg
10   Boneless rolled breast
11   Mock duck
12   Boneless rolled shoulder
13   Saratoga chop

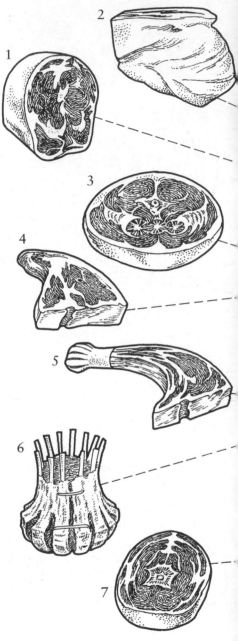

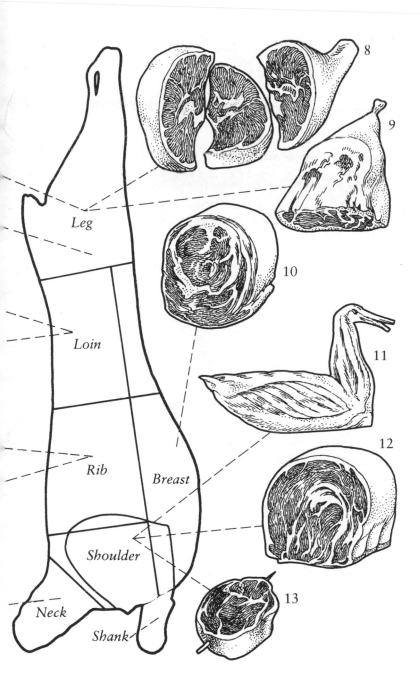

Leg

Loin

Rib

Breast

Shoulder

Neck

Shank

8

9

10

11

12

13

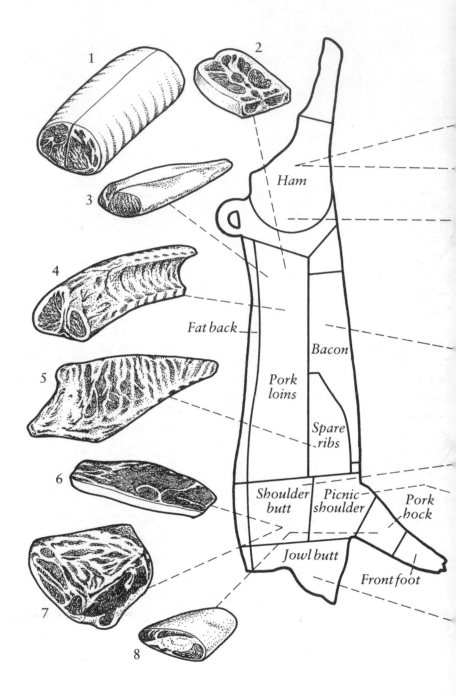

1

2

3

4

5

6

7

8

Ham

Fat back

Bacon

Pork
loins

Spare
ribs

Shoulder
butt

Picnic
shoulder

Pork
hock

Jowl butt

Front foot

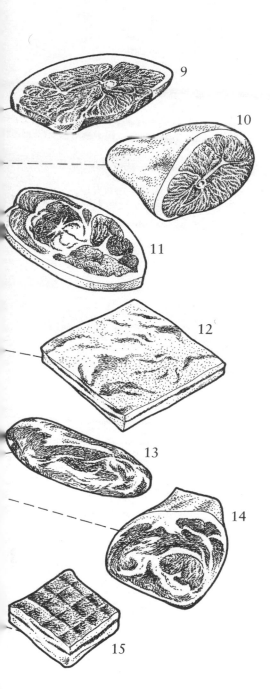

PORK

The American Cuts
Fresh Pork Cuts

1 Boneless ham roast
2 Butterfly pork chop
3 Pork tenderloin
4 Pork loin roast
5 Pork spare ribs
6 Shoulder slice
7 Shoulder butt
8 Pork hock

Smoked Pork Cuts

9 Ham slice (centre cut)
10 Baked ham home-style
11 Ham butt (double slice)
12 Bacon piece
13 Boneless shoulder butt
14 Picnic shoulder
15 Jowl butt

VEAL
The American Cuts

1   Round roast
2   Rump roast
3   Rib chop
4   Rib
5   Shoulder chops
6   Veal birds
7   Round steak
8   Loin steak
9   Loin chop
10   Breast
11   Rolled shoulder
12   'City chicken'

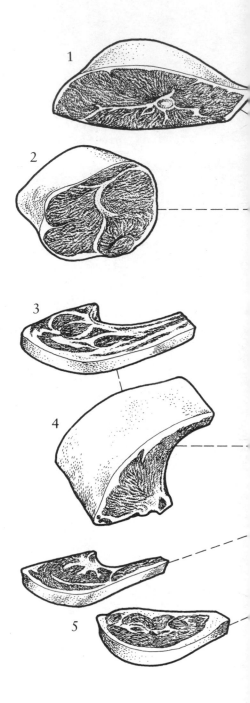

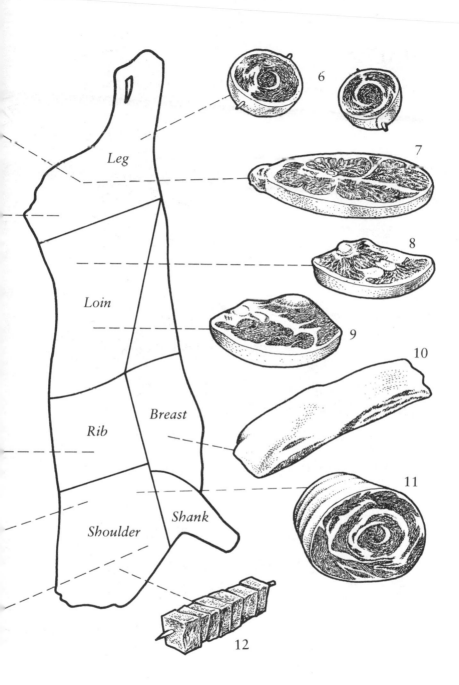

Leg

6

7

Loin

8

9

Rib

Breast

10

11

Shoulder

Shank

12

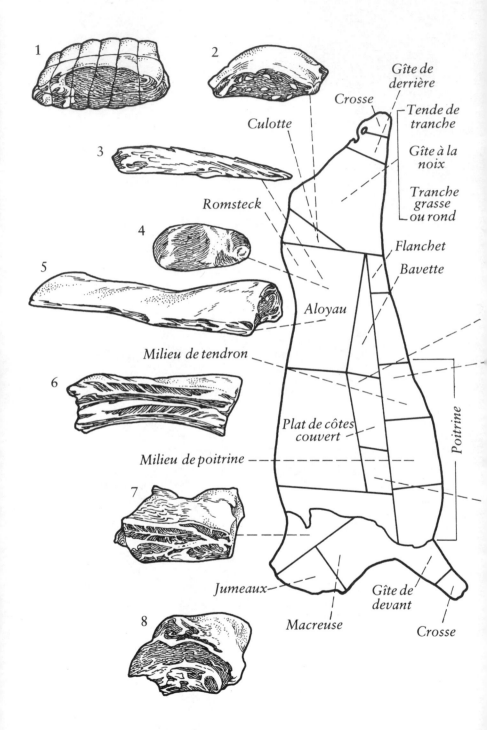

1

2

3

Culotte

Crosse

Gîte de
derrière

Tende de
tranche

Gîte à la
noix

Tranche
grasse
ou rond

Romsteck

4

5

Flanchet

Bavette

Aloyau

Milieu de tendron

6

Plat de côtes
couvert

Milieu de poitrine

Poitrine

7

Jumeaux

Gîte de
devant

8

Macreuse

Crosse

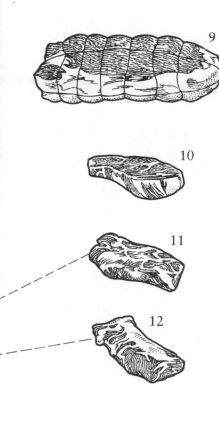

9

BEEF

The French Cuts

1 Contre-filet for roasting
2 Aiguillette
3 Filet
4 Châteaubriand
5 Faux filet (contrefilet)
6 Plat de côte
7 Paleron
8 Poitrine
9 Aloyau for roasting
10 Entrecôte from contrefilet
11 Onglet
12 Hampe
13 Entrecôtes
14 Côtes couvert

10

11

12

13

Plat de côtes découvert

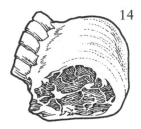

14

LAMB
The French Cuts

1 Gigot d'agneau
2 Gigot
3 Selle d'agneau
4 Côte première
5 Carré
6 Côte seconde
7 Côte découverte
8 Baron d'agneau
9 Côte de filet (mutton chop)
10 Épaule roulée
11 Épaule d'agneau roulée
12 Épaule
13 Épaule d'agneau
14 Épaule roulée en 'ballon'

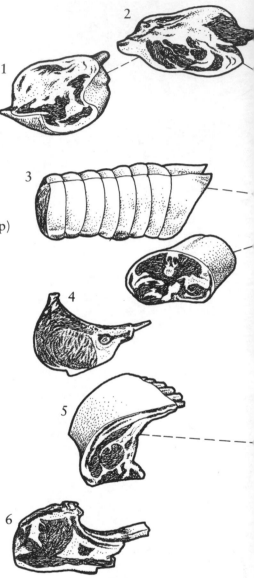

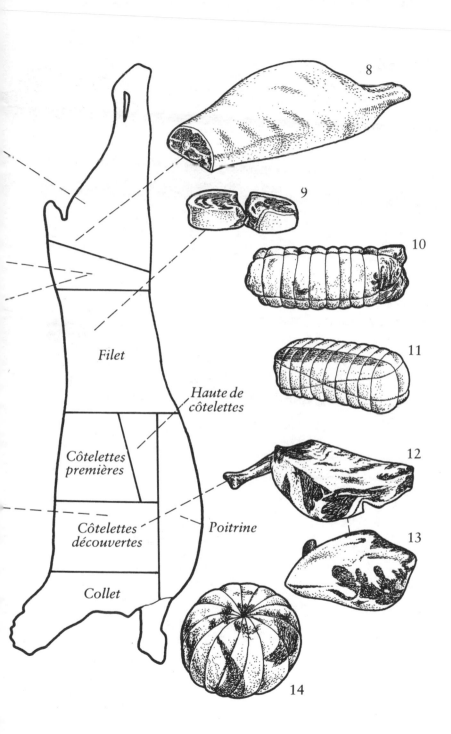

8

9

10

11

Filet

Haute de
côtelettes

Côtelettes
premières

12

Côtelettes
découvertes

Poitrine

13

Collet

14

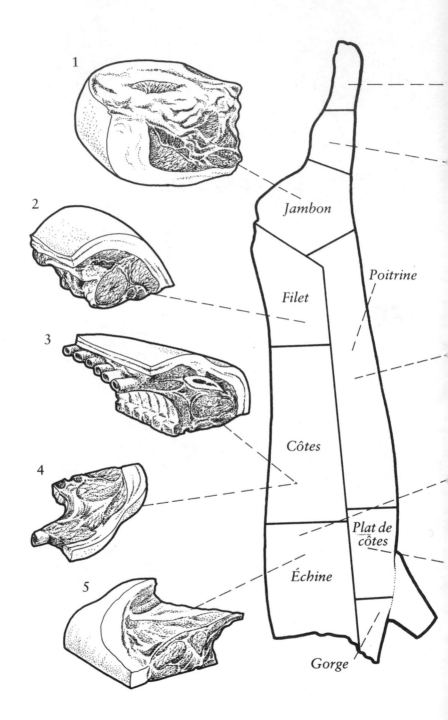

1

2

3

4

5

Jambon

Filet

Côtes

Échine

Poitrine

Plat de côtes

Gorge

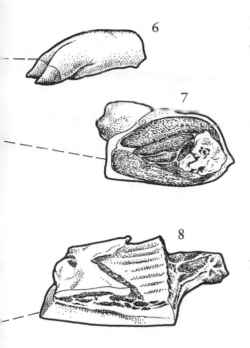

PORK
The French Cuts

1 Jambon
2 Filet
3 Carré
4 Côte
5 Échine
6 Pied
7 Jambonneau
8 Poitrine
9 Palette
10 Plat de côtes

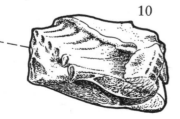

VEAL
The French Cuts

1 Cuisseau (Noix)
2 Carré bardé
3 Carré
4 Escalope
5 Côte
6 Jarret
7 Longe
8 Filet
9 Poitrine (Flanchet)

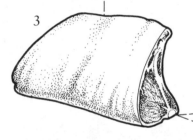

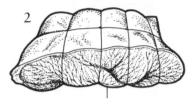

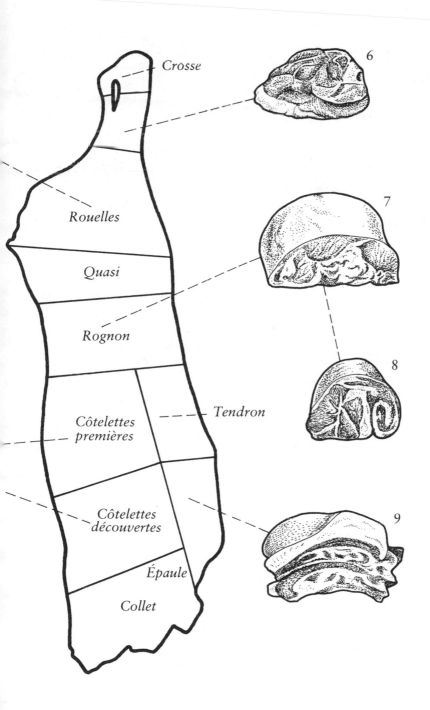

Crosse

6

Rouelles

7

Quasi

Rognon

8

Côtelettes premières

Tendron

Côtelettes découvertes

9

Épaule

Collet

and do not be afraid of giving it a few strokes on the steel at the start, in the middle, or at any time in a carving session, if you think that it is lacking a keen edge.

Please note that the carving illustrations often show the fork inserted in the meat at somewhat odd angles. In an ideal world I suppose the prongs of the fork would be strictly horizontal or parallel to the direction of the path of the knife; in reality a particularly crisp piece of meat or fat can prevent this. 'The best laid plans of mice and men gang after gla' so I am prepared to compromise as long as the food I am carving is firmly secured.

I am sometimes accused of having an unfair advantage over other people who find carving difficult. My critics complain that the meat that they carve does not even look like the meat that I carve; the answer is that I have prepared the joint before cooking it. So I have included a section at the end on Improving on Nature, what you might call kitchen cunning. It is surprising what a difference a skewer or two and some restraining loops of string about a piece of meat or fish can make when carving.

One of the major problems in meat cookery is that there is no agreement between the world's butchers as to the method which should be followed to divide up an animal into the different joints. As you will see from pages 20–43, even the fundamental division of the carcase varies between Britain, France and America; but by checking the position of the particular cut, you can get some guide as to its quality or find a suitable alternative for a particular recipe and the best way of carving it.

It is important to appreciate that the French butcher treats meat as a good tailor treats his cloth and removes fat and gristle before forming it into the particular joint. This applies not only to the prime cuts but even to a piece of leg of beef for the pot-au-feu, which is carefully trimmed and neatly secured with skewers and string before being sold to madame because madame would want to know the reason why if it was not. Perhaps this can give us a guide to our own dealings with our butcher. Tell him when you are pleased with his produce and similarly tell him when you are not. At least he will realize that you can tell the difference.

Meat
Beef

Good beef should be firm but not 'tight' to the touch and the flesh should be a good red with a slight brownish or almost purple caste to the colour and the surface should be moist but not wet.

The flesh should be marbled with small flecks of fat which helps to keep the meat moist and tender while it is cooking. The fat should be creamy white although at some times of the year and depending on the animal's diet it can be almost yellow. (Unfortunately this can also signify that the meat has come from a cow which will make it tough.) In the long run you can only depend on a reliable butcher or supermarket to guarantee that the meat is of good quality.

If the meat has been cut and left exposed to the air for a long time before you have bought it the surface will be dark and dry looking; this can also mean that the meat has come from an older animal. In either case it will be dry and tasteless when it is cooked.

In an ideal world a sirloin should not be less than 2¼ kg (5 lb) and it should be roasted on the bone. In earlier times the sirloin always contained the undercut or fillet and also had the flank attached which was wrapped around the bone to lie against the fillet which protected it during the roasting and kept it moist and underdone. It is as well, however, to check with the butcher or supermarket that the sirloin has the fillet and the flank portion if you want them.

In my opinion the contrefilet is the best cut of beef that one can buy; it makes a small joint of some 1.5–2 kg (3–4 lb). Not cheap, but cheaper and better flavoured than fillet, and there is no waste. Having no fat of its own, if correctly prepared, it requires barding or larding (see pages 106–108). Serve it underdone.

Serving portions
Allow 225 g–350 g (8–12 oz) meat on the bone and about 170 g–225 g (6–8 oz) without bone.

Carving on the bone

The following cuts are the most common on the bone:

Prime Sirloin (Aloyeau) / American standing rib roast / Wing rib / Côtes couvert

Non-prime Top, fore, and back rib / Brisket

1 *Stand the sirloin so that the chine bone is vertical and the undercut is on the underside. Hold it firmly by inserting the prongs into the middle of the meat and then cut down between the meat and the chine bone.*

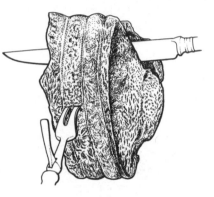

2 *Trim off any pieces of gristle or hard connective tissue at the tip of the meat where it joined the chine bone as it will prevent you from cutting neat slices.*

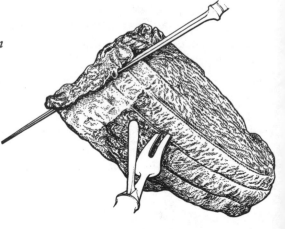

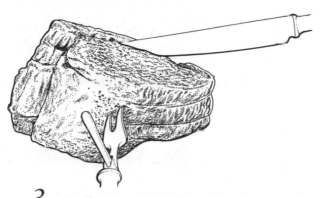

3 Lie the joint on its side and make a cut of about
1 cm (½ in) deep along the rib bone so that the slices will be
freed as you carve them. Note that you can lie the
joint so that the undercut is towards you or facing away from you;
it depends entirely on which you find more convenient.

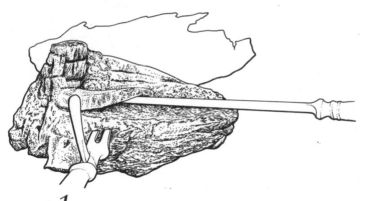

1 Now carve thin slices across the grain of the meat
towards the rib bones. Increase the depth of the cut along the rib
bone after every two or three slices so that they 'fall free of the
knife' as you go. Continue carving thin slices from the sirloin;
note that one cuts along the angle formed by the two bones. I
continue carving in this manner to the end of the sirloin, but some
carvers stand the joint up as shown here when they reach about
half way. They then carve the remaining slices at an increasing
angle so that they avoid having to carve a thin 'wobbly' piece at
the end.

47

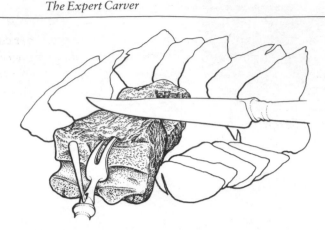

5 Turn the joint around and carve generous slices of the fillet or undercut. Note that the slices are parallel to the grain of the meat; it should be so tender, however, that it is of no importance. Include some of the fillet with each serving and do not forget the fresh horseradish sauce – the commercial variety in jars is a travesty of the real thing.

All other cuts on the bone are carved in a more or less similar way, except they do not have the undercut or fillet; brisket has such a simple bone structure that it can easily be cut free and it is then carved in a similar way to contrefilet (see opposite).

Carving off the bone

The following cuts off the bone are the most common. Note that the Americans call fillet 'tenderloin' and contrefilet 'sirloin'. They are all carved, more or less, as the contrefilet.

Prime Contrefilet / Rolled sirloin or ribs / Fillet / Rolled rump /
Châteaubriand / American chuck roast /
American tenderloin (fillet) / American sirloin (contrefilet) /
American rump roast

Non-prime Top and silverside / Flank / Rolled brisket

There are two methods of carving a contrefilet or any other cut of meat of similar form, such as silverside or boned and rolled joints. Either lay the piece on its side and then cut slices from it almost as if it was a loaf of bread or you may prefer to position it so that the round surface is horizontal and then carve across the grain. I combine both in the following method:

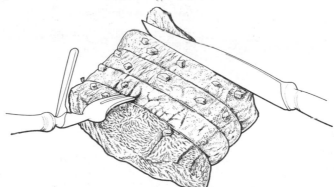

1   Place the joint so that the round surface is vertical and then insert the prongs of the fork into the curved side at the end nearest you, or, if the contrefilet or other meat is particularly long, it might be more convenient to insert the fork nearer the middle, and then carve slices from the far end.

2   When the remaining piece becomes too thin and 'wobbly' to carve, lay it down so that the round surface is horizontal and insert the fork into the side nearest you and carve the remaining slices across the grain, away from the fork, increasing the angle as you come to the end of the piece so that you can carve to the very end.

49

Veal

Veal comes from the immature animal and is therefore softer and moister than beef, but it should not be flabby or wet. The flesh should be of a close texture and the colour should be very pale pink. There should be very little fat and what there is of it should be of a very pale pink to a creamy white. A reasonable quantity of connective tissue, which in an older animal would be gristle, is acceptable, as it softens and almost dissolves during cooking.

Take care if the flesh is mottled or has a brownish or mauve caste to it as this can mean that the meat is stale.

In Italy, where veal is fundamental to many of the great dishes of that country, the meat is classified as to whether it comes from an animal that has not been weaned or one that has fed on grass but has not yet been put to work. In Britain we do not have quite such a fine differentiation so it is advisable to buy veal from a butcher who has a large continental clientele or who has a specialist knowledge of that meat.

Serving portions
Allow 225–350 g (8–12 oz) with bone per portion or, if the proportion of meat to bone is very low, increase the weight to 450 g (16 oz) per portion. When serving a loin allow one to two chops per portion, or two to three cutlets from a best end.

Off the bone, allow 120–170 g (4–6 oz) meat per portion.

Carving on the bone

Prime Leg / Best end of neck / Shoulder / Loin

Carve all the cuts above, more or less, as the equivalent cuts of lamb (see pages 51–63); note, however, that the loin is generally carved with the grain. The shoulder is somewhat large and awkward to carve so it should be boned and rolled; ask your butcher to do it for you or follow the instructions for boning a shoulder of lamb in Improving on Nature, pages 87–88.

Carving off the bone

Prime	Boned and rolled shoulder / American round roast / American rump roast carré bardé
Non-prime	Rolled and stuffed breast

Carve all the cuts off the bone, more or less as contrefilet.

Lamb and Mutton

The flesh will vary from light pink for young lamb to light or dark red for older lamb or mutton; a bluish tinge in the knuckle bones indicates that the animal is very young.

British lamb, which is only available in spring and early summer, should have creamy white fat while imported lamb will have firm white fat. Meat with brittle white fat should be avoided as it can indicate that it has been in the freezer too long. Yellowish fat can be a sign of age.

Legs and shoulders should have a plump look with a thin layer of fat covering the meat. Legs are sometimes divided into two pieces, the leg fillet and the leg knuckle, the leg knuckle being easier to carve. Similarly shoulders are divided into the shoulder blade and the shoulder knuckle, the blade being easier to carve. In both cases one can use the carving technique for the whole joint as a guide to carving the piece.

A saddle of lamb makes a superb dish for a dinner party; a 3.5–4.5 kg (8–10 lb) saddle should feed eight to ten people.

Loin of lamb is somewhat fat, but it is a favourite joint of mine, because the layer of fat keeps it succulent while it is roasting. It is particularly good if one adapts Jane Grigson's recipe for leg of lamb stuffed with crab, in her book *English Food* (Penguin). Do not be alarmed by the combination, it is terrific. Bone the loin and then roll it around the crab forcemeat of which you will require a little more than in the original recipe.

Serving portions
Allow 350 g–450 g (12–16 oz) per portion for meat on the bone, and 120 g–170 g (4–6 oz) for lamb off the bone.

Allow two or three cutlets from a best end and one or two chops from the loin.

Carving on the bone
Whole leg, knuckle and fillet ends
Weight varies from 1.5 kg (3 lb) to 2.5 kg (5 lb) for a whole leg.

You need to know whether you are carving a right or left leg as the thickest meat is on the outer side of the joint and you need to position the joint differently; in the following illustrations I am carving a right leg. If you are carving a left leg you will need to have the knuckle pointing in the other direction and change the angle and direction of the knife accordingly.

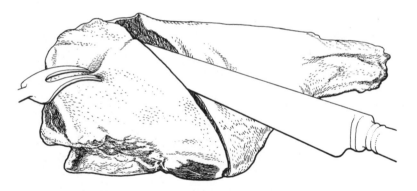

1 Position the joint as shown in (a), steadying it by inserting the prongs of the fork into the joint towards the left. Note that the pelvic bone is on the underside and also note the position of the bones as they dictate the limits of the slices that one can cut from any particular part of the joint. Make the first cut by inserting the knife on the far side of the joint and cutting through to the bone and levelling the knife to be almost parallel to the plate as shown.

52

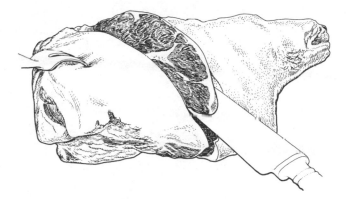

2 *Make a second cut a little over ½ cm (¼ in) to the left and then, by changing the angle of the knife almost parallel to the bone, remove the first slice.*

3 *Continue carving slices towards the knuckle, changing the angle of the knife slightly to get larger slices, releasing them after every two or three, by changing the angle of the knife as you did for the first slice. When you have carved as many slices as you can the joint will look like this.*

4 *Turn the joint over, steady it with the fork as shown, and make the first cut more or less in the same position as you did when you started carving the leg. Continue carving slices towards the knuckle, releasing them, as you did on the first side, by changing the angle of the knife and cutting parallel to the bone.*

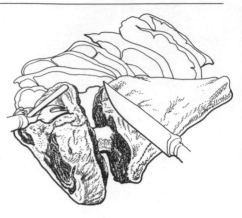

5 *Note that as you get nearer the knuckle the distribution of the meat changes and you need to change the angle of the knife to carve reasonable slices as the bone does not lie in the exact centre of the joint.*

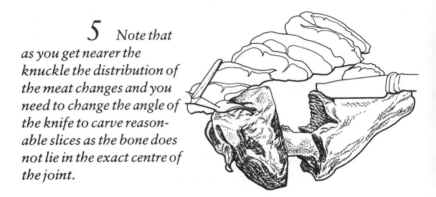

Shoulder, shoulder blade and shoulder knuckle
Weight varies from just over 1 kg to 1.5 kg (2½–3½ lb) for a whole shoulder.

As with the leg you need to know whether you are carving a right or left shoulder and position it accordingly and also change the angle of the various cuts. The following illustrations show a right shoulder. If you are carving a left shoulder you will need to have the knuckle facing in the other direction and you will also need to change the angle and direction of the knife accordingly.

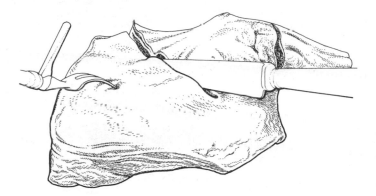

1 *Try to feel the position of the blade bone before you cook the meat so that you can make the first cut as near to the blade as possible. Insert the prongs of the fork into the fleshy part of the shoulder just above the blade bone, make a deep cut from the edge of the shoulder furthest away from you and then continue the cut until you hit the bone and then lower the handle of the knife so that the blade is almost parallel to the plate.*

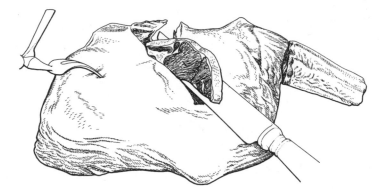

2 *Make a second cut a little over ½ cm (¼ in) from the first and remove the slice by changing the angle of the knife to almost parallel with the bone. Continue removing slices until the bone has been cleared, changing the angle of the carving knife as you get closer to the knuckle.*

55

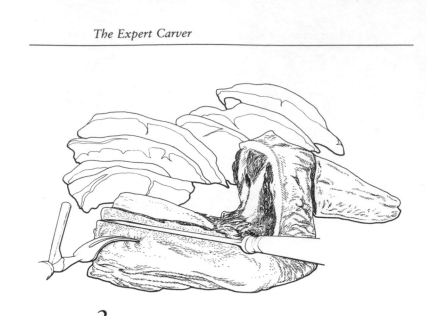

3   Change the position of the fork and insert the prongs into the edge of the meat above the blade bone. Now carve the meat from the blade. Note that the slices will be only half the thickness of the rest.

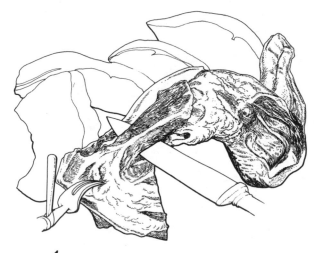

4   Now turn the shoulder over and, holding it with the fork in the position shown, carve thin slices from the other side.

5   *When you have finished carving as much meat off the blade as you can, change the position of the fork and carve short slices from the knuckle, carving at a slight angle to increase the size of the slices.*

Loin of lamb

Ensure that the loin has been chined. While obviously the loin can come from either the left or right side of the animal it does not make as much difference to the carving of the joint as it does to the leg or shoulder.

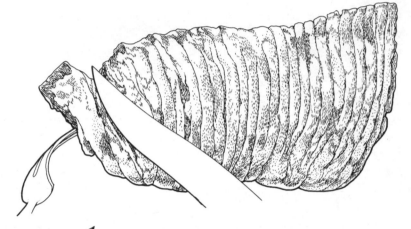

1   Place the loin on the plate so that the chump end is away from you. Insert the fork into the end nearest you and cut along the rib bone to release the first cutlet. Continue dividing the loin into chops until you reach the chump, if your joint includes it.

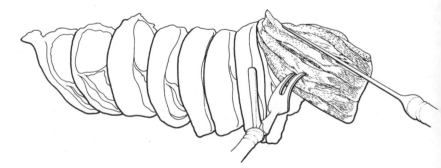

2   Anchor the chump with the fork and then, tilting it slightly, carve diagonal slices from it.

Saddle of lamb

There are two ways of carving the saddle; one can either remove the entire fillet from both sides of the saddle and then cut them into slices or one carves along the first parallel to the grain of the meat. With the latter method you obviously have to divide the strips of fillet into convenient lengths for serving; the former method is particularly good if one wants to carve the joint in the kitchen and then reconstitute it with some form of garnish or filling inserted between the slices. The following description and illustrations show one side of the saddle carved using the first method, on the other the second.

1 *Cut along the entire length of one side of the middle ridge of the saddle, steadying the joint by inserting the fork in the side nearest you. Slide the knife along and under the whole fillet to release it and lay it on the plate.*

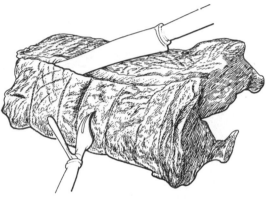

2 *Cut slices of about ½ cm (¼ in) thick across the grain of the fillet.*

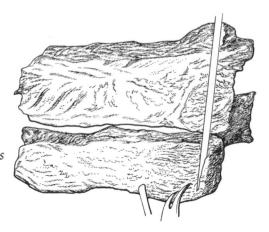

59

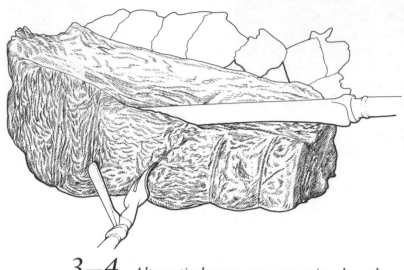

3—4 *Alternatively, you can carve strips along the length of the fillet about ½ cm (¼ in) thick and then into convenient lengths for serving. Release the strips either by changing the angle of the knife and cutting under each strip and towards the bone or by cutting horizontally under the fillet when you have finished cutting the whole of it into strips.*

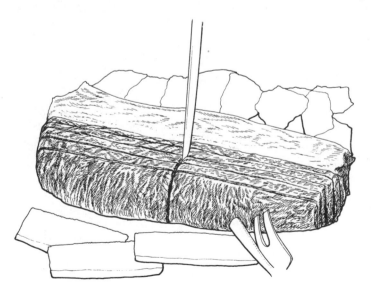

Best end

Make sure that the joint has been chined, or that the chine bone has been cut between each cutlet.

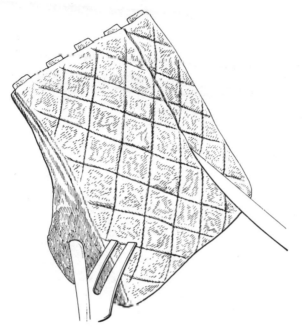

5   *Cut along each rib bone to divide the joint into separate cutlets or groups of cutlets; however, if the joint has not been chined it will be necessary to cut between the chine bone relating to each cutlet or group of cutlets.*

Crown roast

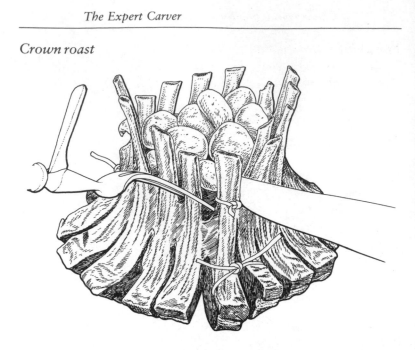

1 As you will see from pages 98–99, the crown roast is made from two or more best ends and is, therefore, carved as the best end. Take care, however, if it is filled with new potatoes or small glazed onions because you may release an avalanche when you cut through the first cutlet or the string holding the crown together.

Carré d'agneau
Carve this as the best end.

Carving off the bone

Prime	Rolled loin / Rolled shoulder or 'en ballon'
Non-prime	Rolled and stuffed breast

All the cuts off the bone are carved, more or less, as a contrefilet (see page 49).

Boned and rolled shoulder

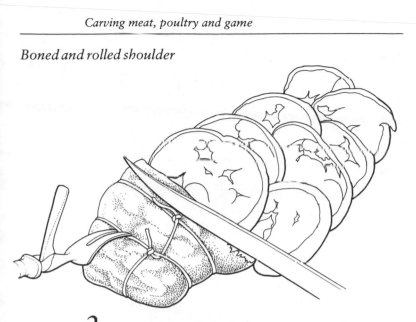

2 *It is as well with a boned and rolled shoulder to leave the strings in position until you have actually reached the point they are securing, as they help to hold the joint together. Cut a slice from one end. Continue carving until you have almost reached the end of the roll. Changing the position of the fork allows you to tilt the remaining piece of meat to enable you to carve to the very last slice.*

Pork

Good quality pork should be slightly moist to the touch and be a nice pale pink; a deeper rose red is a sign of an older animal. Obviously if a larger joint is required a compromise has to be made between the size of the animal and its quality. A brownish tinge to the flesh is an indication of staleness or age.

The fat should be firm and a good creamy white; poor quality pork has off-white, soft and 'oily' fat.

Unfortunately the modern trend is to produce pork with very little fat, but a good layer of fat is a sign of quality. The rind should be thin and soft; if the meat has not been stored under good conditions or it has been stored too long the skin will be dry and hard. Thick and roughened skin is a sign of age.

Serving portions
Allow 225–350 g (8–12 oz) per portion when serving a leg of pork, hand and spring, spare ribs or blade.

Allow one chop per portion from a loin, although it is advisable to have a few extra so that the servings do not look too precise; anyway cold pork is delicious so who would complain?

To prepare pork before cooking see Improving on Nature, page 103.

Carving

Prime   Loin / Leg and half leg
Non-prime   Hand and spring

Loin
Carve as a loin of lamb.

Leg and half leg
Both are carved more or less as the equivalent joint of lamb. The various supermarket 'pork leg roll joints' are carved horizontally across the grain, the half circle slices coming from either side of the central bone. You might find it convenient to rotate the joint so that you always carve towards the bone.

Hand and spring
While this cut is not prime it can be very good eating if it is braised on a bed of aromatic vegetables; remove the lid of the pan for the last half hour or so to allow the crackling to become crisp.

See page 103 for an illustration of how the fat of the hand and spring should be cut into thin strips before cooking. This will aid the carving.

1 Note that
*the joint almost forms a T
about the knuckle. Place
the hand and spring so that
the knuckle is on the right
side. Insert the fork into
the middle of the joint and
then carve slices from
either of the arms of the T.*

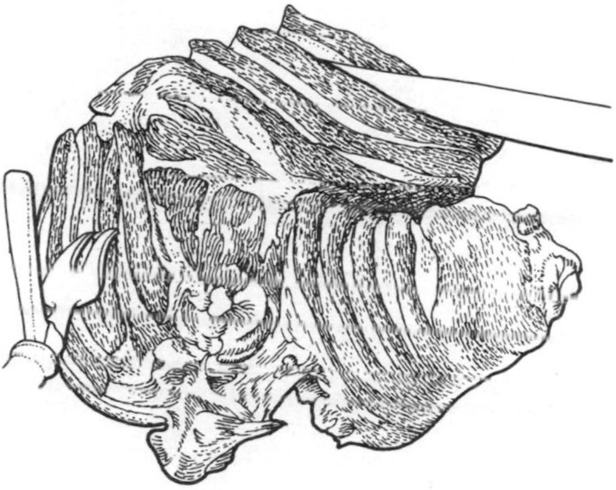

2 Turn the
*joint around and then
carve the other arm of the
T.*

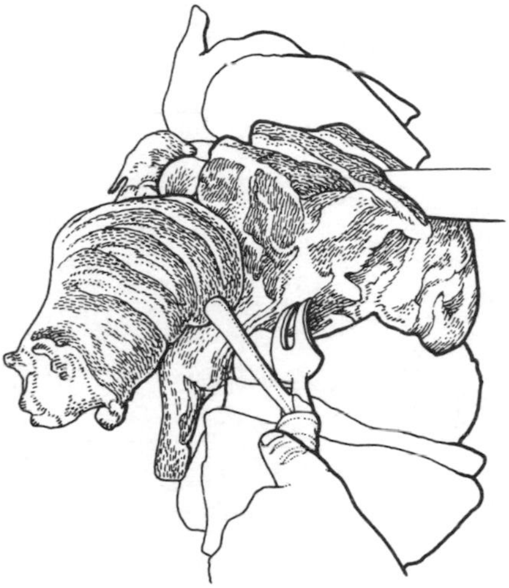

3 Finish by
*carving the meat off the
knuckle; angle the knife so
that the slices are not too
narrow.*

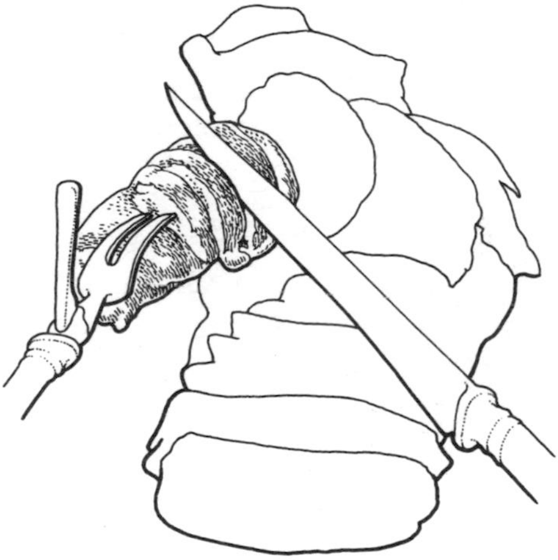

65

Miscellaneous

Boar's head

The boar's head of the Edwardian period was more for effect than nourishment, although its appearance is still a ritual at large functions. An average head only provides about 2 kg (4½ lb) of meat. The modern equivalent is a boned pig's head filled with a rich, truffled forcemeat and then honey-glazed and served cold. The carving of the finished product is simply a matter of cutting thin slices from the back of the head.

Sucking pig

The style of serving this dish will depend on your own sensibilities and on consideration of your guest's feelings. I always think of the scenario 'Three little piglets went to market' with a touch of the 'Agatha Christie's' as a sub plot. I must admit that as much as I like eating sucking pig I find its appearance, bedecked with flowers, fruit, and garlands of leaves about its neck, and its staring, scarlet, cranberried eyes, somewhat unsettling. I would prefer it to be carved and served out of sight.

You will find an electric carving knife simplifies the carving of this dish as the crackling is normally not cut into strips before cooking; and certainly poultry shears help to cut through the joints effortlessly.

1 Cut the
skin around the shoulder
and then insert the point of
the knife and cut through
the joints; the pig should
be well cooked so that the
front leg should come
away easily. If, however, it
resists your efforts use
poultry shears to cut
through the joint.

2 Cut the
skin around the hind leg
and remove the leg.
Remove the legs from the
other side.

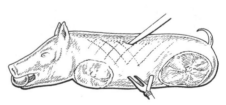

3 Cut the
crackling into convenient
sized squares for serving,
using poultry shears or an
electric carving knife if you
have them, or break it by
tapping it with the knife
and then cutting it free of
the fat and meat below.

4 Carve the
rest of the pig as if it were
saddle of lamb, as most of
the meat lies along the loin
and the equivalent of the
best end.

American boneless ham roast and rolled loin
Carve these cuts as you would a contrefilet (see page 49).

Gammon hock

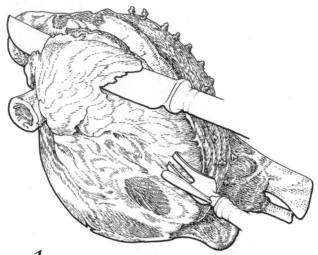

1   *Place the gammon hock with the narrow knuckle end pointing away from you and the meatiest side of the gammon uppermost. Insert the fork into the lower half of the wide end facing you and carve the first slice at a slight angle off the vertical.*

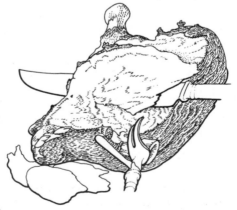

2   *Continue carving slices off the gammon, flattening the knife as you come nearer the knuckle so that the slices are not too narrow.*

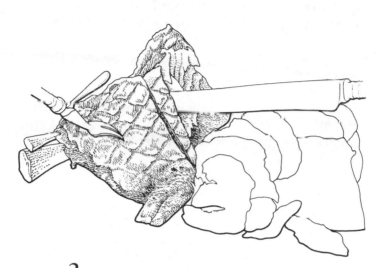

3 Turn the joint over and carve the other side;
alternatively you may prefer to have the knuckle nearest you for
carving this side. Finally, if you are using the whole joint carve
any remaining pieces of meat from the bone; do not be too
concerned if these last bits are not perfectly shaped as they will be
from the nooks and crannies of the gammon, as it were.

All other cuts of bacon or pork, such as middle hock or the
supermarket 'pork roast', containing a small piece of bone in the
centre, can be carved in a more or less similar manner to the
gammon hock.

Middle gammon, gammon slipper, corner gammon, fore hock,
fore slipper, butt, shoulder and collar cuts
These are all carved as any boned cut; but remember to carve
across the grain when dealing with any of the 'corner' cuts such as
corner gammon, slipper or butt.

Poultry
Chicken and Capon

Modern farming has produced the supermarket chicken retailing at a very economical price but unfortunately the flavour is also economical so one should add forcemeats, vegetables, herbs and spices to make good the lack. For a special occasion buy poultry either from a farm or a supplier of free-range birds and use the following points as a guide to quality; they can also, obviously, be used for prepackaged birds if you are able to inspect the bird through the wrapping. The breast should be plump and firm to the touch, the tip of the breast bone should be reasonably soft and pliable and the leg scales should be small. If the bird is a cock the spurs should be only partly developed.

A capon is a young cock that has been emasculated by knife or hormone treatment and, therefore, has the attributes of a Renaissance castrato – it is plump and fleshy. They weigh from 3.5–4.5 kg (8–10 lb) The breast meat should be deep and of firm texture, but the bird should not have run to fat.

Serving portions
A 1.5 kg (3½ lb) chicken, containing a bread stuffing and forcemeat, should provide four to five portions. Allow a similar weight of capon as chicken per serving portion.

Carving
Ensure that the carving knife is well sharpened and then remove any trussing string or skewers.

It is good practice to carve as much meat as will be required for the first service. This prevents other guests' portions from getting cold while everyone is being served; it also allows you to assess whether portions need to be limited. This is particularly important if you have been press-ganged, as a guest, into carving someone else's offering, burnt or otherwise!

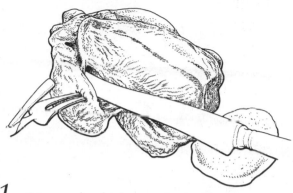

1   *Line up the chicken as shown if you are right-handed. (If you are left-handed you may have to reverse all the positions.)*

If the chicken has sausage meat or a similar forcemeat inserted between the skin and the flesh at the neck end, start by steadying the chicken by inserting the prongs of the fork on either side of the breast bone and then cut thin slices of the forcemeat and arrange them at each end of the plate. Insert the prongs of the fork into the thick part of the drumstick and with gentle pressure lever it away from the body to allow you to cut through the skin.

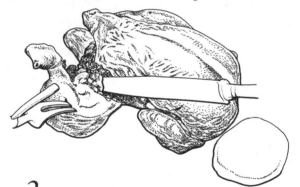

2   *Insert the prongs of the fork into the inside of the drumstick and, bearing downwards, force the drumstick away from the body so that you can see the joint. Insert the point of the knife into the joint and cut through it. If it resists your attentions, you can use poultry shears to cut through the joints (see the illustration on page 74).*

71

3 Separate
the drumstick from the
thigh by cutting through
the joint, making two
portions. If the bird is very
large, you might prefer to
carve slices off them.

Turn the bird around
and remove the other
drumstick using a similar
technique.

4 Now
remove the wings taking
care to cut as close to the
joint as possible so as not
to remove any of the
breast.

5 Lay the
bird on its side and cut thin
slices from the breast
starting the first slice from
almost the point of the
wing joint, steadying the
fowl by inserting the
prongs of the fork just
beneath the breast bone.

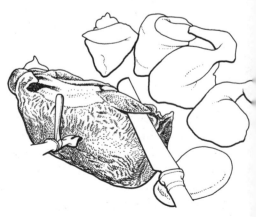

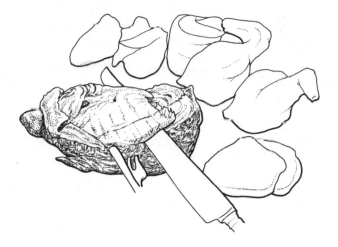

6 *As you get closer to the breast bone you will need to change the angle at which you are holding the knife so that it follows the contours of the carcass.*

If the bird has been overcooked it is almost impossible to carve the breast neatly as it is likely to disintergrate. You will find it easier to remove the breast in one piece and then cut it into slices on the flat surface of the carving platter. Remove the breast by making a vertical incision parallel to the breast bone and then sliding the knife between the breast and the carcass, gently forcing the meat away in one piece.

If the bird contains forcemeat use a long-handled spoon to scoop it out. Serve a portion of both brown and white meat to each guest, as well as any forcemeat, stuffing, bacon rolls or other garnishes.

Turkey

If you remember that carving a turkey is almost identical to carving a chicken (see pages 71–73) you can gain valuable experience throughout the year in preparation for the Christmas bird. You will notice that I do not carve poultry in the traditional manner; I have chosen the easiest route to produce good slices of breast with the least effort.

The breast should be plump and the flesh below the skin should be white with a slight blue caste; some suppliers dust the bird with flour so take care when choosing your bird that its colour is its own and not cosmetic.

Serving portions
Allow 300–350 g (10–12 oz) per serving.

Poussin

To serve a poussin, split the bird in two with poultry shears as described below. Each bird will serve one person.

1 *Insert the point of the shears into the opening between the drumsticks and then cut through the breast bone.*

2 *Cut through the underside of the carcass and separate the two halves.*

Duck

Domestic ducks are available throughout the year but are at their best during June and July. (Wild duck, of course, belong to the game season and are at their best early in the season, August and September). Choose a bird with a good plump breast, and in a young bird the beak and breast bone will be flexible.

Serving portions
The breast meat is very shallow so a 1.5 kg (3–3½ lb) duck will only serve two to three portions.

Carving

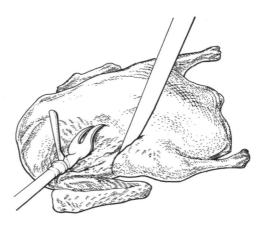

1 *Anchor the bird by pushing the prongs of the forks into the side of the breast. Note that the leg of the duck lies much closer to the body than that of the chicken so it is necessary to cut through the skin before forcing the whole leg away from the bird so that one can reach the joint.*

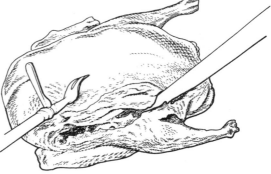

2 *Use the blade of the knife to lever the leg away from the bird and then cut through the joint.*

75

3 Hold the drumstick firmly with the fork while you cut through the 'knee' joint making two portions of the drumstick and the thigh.

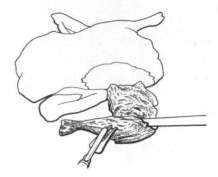

4 Lever the wing away from the body with the fork and then cut through the joint. Remove the leg and wing from the other side of the bird.

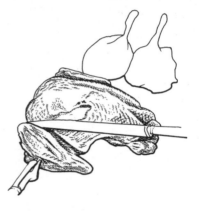

5 Roll the bird on to its side and carve thin slices of the breast, starting the first slice from the point where you removed the wing. Depending on the thickness of the breast you will need to change the angle of the knife, sooner or later, to follow the contours of the bones so that you will be able to carve good slices of the remaining breast.

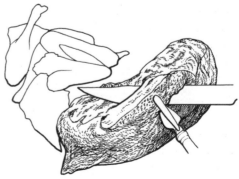

Goose

Fortunately, for those of us who prefer goose to turkey, they are at their best at Christmas in the Northern hemisphere, but are in season from September until February. When choosing a larger bird ensure that the scales on the legs are soft and yellow and that the legs still have down growing on them.

Take care that the goose has not run to fat as there will be little extra meat for the additional weight.

Serving portions
You will need a 4.5 kg (10 lb) goose to get eight portions as, like duck, the breast is shallow.

Carving
The anatomy of a goose is very similar to the duck, both having a fairly shallow breast and a similar articulation of the leg joint, so you can carve one like the other. Follow the instructions above for carving a duck.

Game
Rabbit and Hare

Wild rabbits and hares are at their best from early autumn to the end of February. The claws should be smooth and the cleft in the lip should be small. The ears should tear easily. Rely on a good game dealer to ensure that your hare or rabbit is of good quality and has been hung for the correct time. It is advisable to marinate wild rabbit and hare and then lard them before cooking as the flesh is inclined to be dry.

Serving portions
A good wild rabbit of some 1.5 kg (3 lb) will provide five or six portions; a young hare, or leveret, of about 3 kg (6 lb) will serve six to eight people.

Carving

Our Edwardian great-grandparents were inclined to serve hare or rabbit with the skill of the American mortician in Evelyn Waugh's *The Loved One*. Fortunately the fashion has passed and they generally appear in convenient portions suitable for serving. However, if you are faced with one lying on a bed of watercress, smiling up at you, with its ears gracefully arranged behind its head, as if it was in its favourite field . . . I suggest you follow the procedure below instead of greeting it as Flopsy Bunny.

Remove the front and hind legs on either side of the body and divide them into two portions each and then carve the rest as a miniature saddle of lamb.

Venison

Venison from the buck is in season from July until late September and is considered to be of better quality than that from the doe. Doe venison has a slightly longer season, from late June until early January. Like most game, venison should be hung for a period and unless you have the space, time and knowledge of when it was shot it is advisable to rely on your supplier. As the meat is very lean it is as well to marinate it for a few days in a cool place and lard it before cooking. Braise rather than roast it. Fillets of venison, if of good quality, can be sautéed and are delicious.

Serving portions

Allow 225–300 g (8–10 oz) of venison off the bone and 350–450 g (12–16 oz) on the bone.

Carving

Leg, loin, saddle and shoulder of venison are dealt with in much the same way as the equivalent cuts of lamb or mutton.

Large birds carved as poultry

The legs should be fairly supple and the leg scales small and smooth. If the bird is a cock, the spurs should be short. The feathers on the breast and the area under the wings should be soft and downy. The wing feathers should be pointed; rounded wing feathers are a sign of old age and the bird will be tough and dry unless casseroled.

Black game
In season from late August to early December. Allow one between three or four people depending on its size.

Pheasant
In season from mid August to the end of January. A hen pheasant, which is more succulent and of better flavour than the cock, will feed two or three people. A cock will feed three or four.

Wild duck
In season from early August to the end of February. Allow one bird between two or three people, but take care as the breast is shallow and should be the only portion served.

Guinea fowl
Now available in Great Britain more or less the whole year around since they have become domesticated. A 1.2–1.5 kg (2½–3 lb) bird will serve four people.

Single or two-portion birds

Grouse
In season from the Glorious Twelfth of August until 10 December. Allow one young grouse per person. An older grouse at the end of the season needs casseroling and can serve two, in which case see the instructions for dividing a poussin on page 74.

Woodcock

These are at their best during November and December, generally roasted undrawn after hanging for a short period. A good woodcock should serve two people. Like snipe, they should be roasted on a slice of bread, which has been fried on one side, so that the juices will be saved as they cook. Place the uncooked bird on the soft surface of the bread. When the bird is cooked, carve off each breast and leg in one piece and serve on half a slice of the bread, on which it was cooked.

Alternatively the bird can be split into two with poultry shears (see the instructions for poussin on page 74). The trail is considered a delicacy by some and can be spread on the bread.

Pigeon

They are particularly good at harvest time but are in season all the year around. Allow one pigeon per serving unless they are very large and your guests' appetites very small. See the instructions for dividing a poussin on page 74.

Quail

Available all year around in Britain as a result of quail farming. Allow one per serving.

Snipe

Snipe are migratory birds in season from early September to the end of February. Cook undrawn, so follow the serving instructions for woodcock, but as snipe are small one will be required per serving.

Partridge

Partridge are in season from early September to the end of January. A partridge should provide two servings, particularly if they are past their prime, and braised with a selection of aromatic vegetables.

Teal

One of the smallest wild duck and in season from early September until the end of January but at their best before Christmas. Serve one per person.

Charcuterie
Salted Tongue

Tongue can be served hot or cold. Carving the finished dish is the same for either on condition that the tongue has been correctly prepared before cooking (see the instructions on preparing a tongue in Improving on Nature, page 110).

Rely on a reputable supplier for your tongue as there are no obvious signs of good quality. However, having said that, if the stock in which it is cooking becomes very salty early in the cooking period, it would be worth changing the water, and adding another lot of aromatic vegetables before cooking continues.

Carving

1 Insert the prongs of the fork into the near-side half of the roll. Cut the first slice from the tongue at a slight angle to the horizontal. Continue carving, increasing the angle as you go, tending almost to 45° when there is about 3 cm (1½ in) left of the tongue, so that you will be able to carve good slices to the last piece.

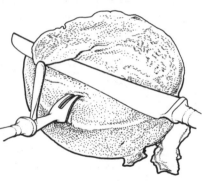

2 Change the angle and position of the fork to cut the last few slices. You might even find it more convenient to turn the fork upside down so that the curve of the prongs does not get in your way; take care the knife does not slip as the guard will not be in the correct position to protect you.

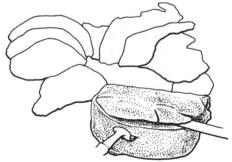

81

Haggis and Saucisson

Both these delicacies are simple to carve, if one can describe the process as carving. Cut them into slices, the thickness of which should depend on the texture and the cross section of the filling. Do not forget to serve plenty of neeps and tatties with the haggis.

Fish

The skin should be shiny, the flesh firm and springy and the lower part of the body and tail relatively rigid. The eyes should be full, bright and glossy. Any blood in the body cavity or gills should be a good red and the fish should smell fresh. Remember, however, that fish of the skate family such as skate, shark and rays smell of ammonia for a couple of days immediately after being killed; they should not be cooked until this odour has almost disappeared. Any remaining ammonia will then be driven off by the cooking process. Always ask the fishmonger to fillet fish for you rather than buying fillets off the slab, as they are likely to be stale. By following the instructions in Improving on Nature, pages 120–124, you can fillet your own.

Fish (such as salmon, sea trout and cod)

Always lace up the abdomen of a fish if it has been cut open for cleaning to prevent it from gaping when it is cooked. Follow the instructions at the end of Filleting a Mackerel on pages 122–124.

Whether you decide to remove the skin of the fish before serving it is entirely a matter of your own preference and the amount of time you have at your disposal. I remove the skin if I intend serving it cold and leave the skin on if I am serving it hot. I think that hot fish is inclined to become dry if the skin is removed unless it is masked with a sauce or gratin. I coat the cold fish with two or three layers of well-flavoured aspic; any decoration should be carried out with a very light hand otherwise the poor fish looks more like an overdressed pearly king or queen than something to eat.

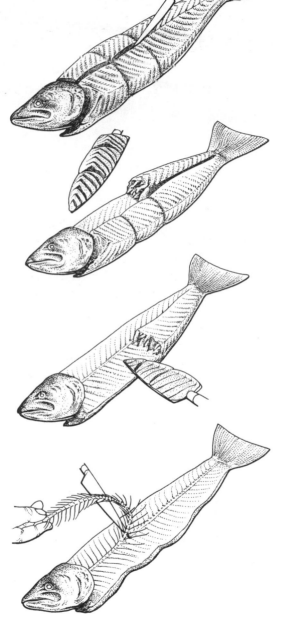

1 Serve the other half of the fillet similarly, by loosening it from the rib bones and cutting it into suitable portions.

3 Cut along the spine of the fish.

2 Lift up the tail and carefully remove the spine and then serve the rest of the fish.

4 Slide the blade of the knife under the fillet to loosen it and then cut it across to give reasonable serving portions.

Improving
on nature

Boning, chining, rolling and fancy work

Boning a joint might deny the cook the opportunity of demonstrating new-found skills as an expert carver, but some recipes require it and it certainly saves time and effort when it comes to serving the ravening hordes.

Chining separates the back bone from the ribs in the relevant joint and makes for easier carving when dealing with best end of lamb or ribs of beef.

Fancy work covers all those procedures that produce meat in a more decorative or convenient form than has come from the 'hoof'.

Boning a leg of lamb or mutton

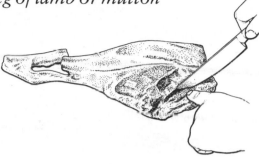

1 Cut along the somewhat convoluted line of the top of the hip bone and then free it by cutting along the underside, taking care to keep the end of the joint as neat as possible.

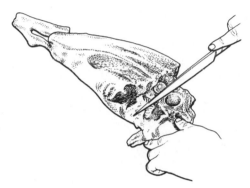

2 Roll the meat back and cut the tendons attaching it to the ball joint of the main leg bone.

3 Remove the hip bone and roll the meat further away from the main thigh bone to reach the next ball and socket joint, using a knife to cut and scrape the meat away from the bone. Use the point of the knife to separate the meat as you twist the bone back and forwards to allow you to see the ball joint at the other end.

4 *Cut*
through the external
tendons of the joint
and then through the
knee joint itself and
remove the bone.

5 *Then*
cut off the end of the
shank bone but leave
the rest of the shank
bone in situ to keep
the 'leg of mutton'
shape. Re-arrange
the leg, bringing the
edges of the joint
together and securing
them with short
skewers. Finish off by
crosslacing the
skewers with string.
Cook it as you wish,
removing the skewers
and string before
serving.

Note: Even if you do not wish to bone the leg completely, carving
is made very much more simple by removing the hip joint and
skewering and crosslacing the gap.

Boning a shoulder of lamb

1 Lay the shoulder with skin-side downwards and cut the meat away from the blade bone.

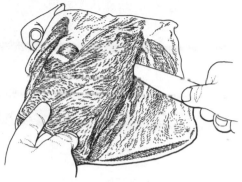

2 Cut the meat away from the underside of the blade bone.

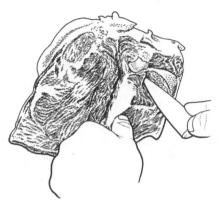

3 Cut through the joint and remove the blade bone.

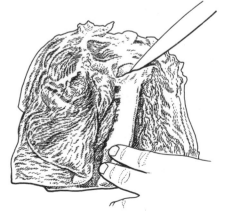

4 *Free the main bone of the shoulder by cutting and scraping the meat away with the knife.*

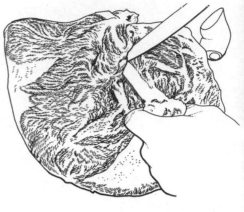

5 *Cut through the joint and remove the bone.*

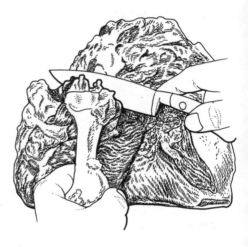

6 *The boned shoulder ready for rolling or preparing 'en ballon'.*

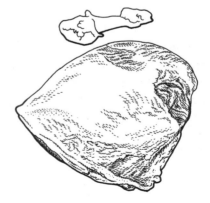

Preparing a shoulder 'en ballon'

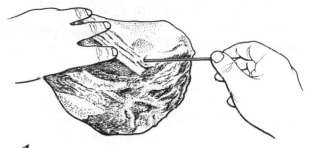

1 Lay the boned shoulder with the skin on the underside. Pull one of the corners of the joint into the centre and secure with a skewer.

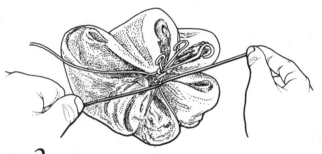

2 Do the same with the other four corners and tuck in the remains of the shank and secure them by tying a loop of string around the 'ballon'.

3 Turn the joint over and continue tying loops of string at even spaces around the ballon, tying a knot at the crossover point on each side as you go, until you have a finished 'ballon'.

89

Preparing a shoulder as a rolled joint

1 Lie the boned shoulder with the skin side underneath and wrap the two longest edges together and secure them with skewers.

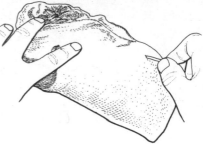

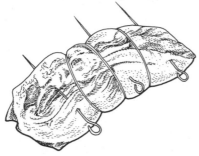

2 Turn the joint over and tie loops of string around the roll at 2 cm (1 in) intervals, ensuring that the knots are on top. Trim the string neatly and cook as directed in the recipe.

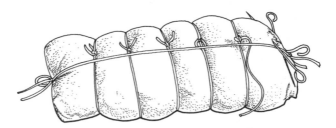

3 Insert skewers at either side of the roll and tie a loop of string around them and on either side of the length of the roll to prevent it from curling up when it is cooked.

Stuffing

It is possible to fill the resulting cavity of the leg, roll or the 'ballon' with a small quantity of forcemeat before forming it into the required shape. Fill the cavity in the leg or spread the forcemeat evenly over the surface of the shoulder and then follow the instructions for tying and finishing off. I, however, prefer to use a rolled loin or best end of lamb when I want to prepare a joint containing forcemeat, as the resulting cavity is larger and its capacity is more or less even for the length of the roll.

Boning a chicken

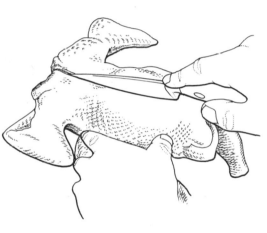

1 *Lay the chicken breast downwards and make a cut through the skin and flesh from the neck to the tail along the backbone. Cut off the parson's nose.*

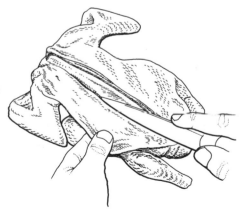

2 *Ease the skin and flesh away from the carcass and, keeping the blade of the knife pointing towards the bone, gently cut the flesh away.*

91

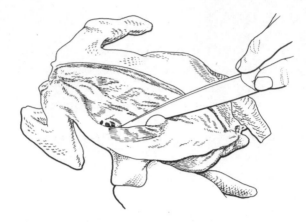

$3-4$ *Cut through the wing and leg joints, taking care not to pierce the skin. You will find it easier if you move the leg or wing around a few times to see how the joint fits together; then you can position the knife accurately to cut through the joint only.*

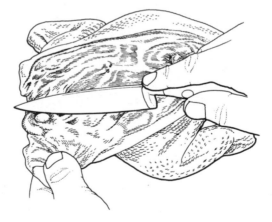

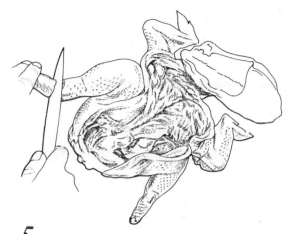

5 Remove the foot joint from the leg and push the bones of the leg towards the body while holding the skin of the leg in the other hand to force the thigh bone out of the skin, turning the leg inside out as you do so. Use the knife to cut away the flesh from the thigh bone and then continue to free the drumstick.

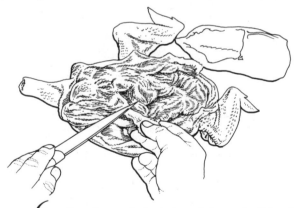

6 Cut through the joint at the end of the drumstick, and also the wing joint. There is no need to bone the wing as there is very little flesh on the bones and leaving them complete contributes to the illusion that the completely boned chicken is just a normal roast fowl. Take particular care when you are cutting through the wing joint as it is very easy to pierce the skin. Bone the thigh and drumstick and cut through the wing joint on the other side.

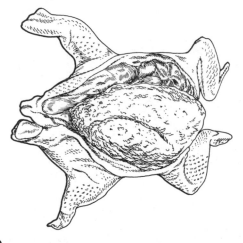

7 *Remove the rib cage and the rest of the carcass by lifting it and cutting it free of the breast meat.*

8 *Place the forcemeat in the centre of the chicken and bring the skin up and over it securing it with short skewers. Use two longer skewers to secure the wings and legs in the correct position.*

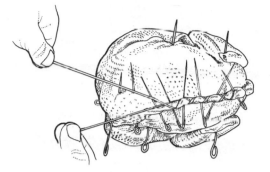

9   *Starting with a loop of string, use it to cross over between each skewer to prevent the bird from bursting while it is cooking.*

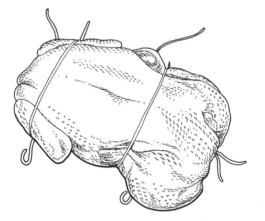

10   *Place the bird, breast side uppermost, the cut side underneath, on a lightly oiled tray from a fish or ham kettle and cook initially in simmering water, before finishing it in a hot oven to brown it, or follow the instructions in your recipe. When the bird is cooked, slide it on to a heated serving plate and gently remove the skewers and release the string.*

Fancy work with best end of lamb
Preparing noisettes

1 *Lay the joint with the ribs on the underside and then cut down the chine bone (the half of the spine with the narrow channel in the middle).*

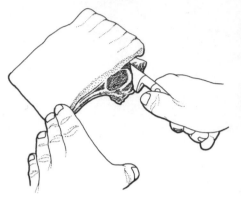

2 *Cut along the cutlet bones keeping the blade of the knife to the line of the bone.*

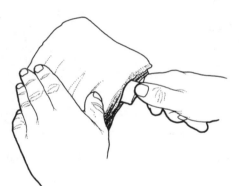

3 *Remove the fibrous skin, and excess fat if necessary.*

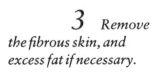
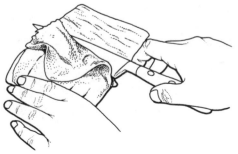

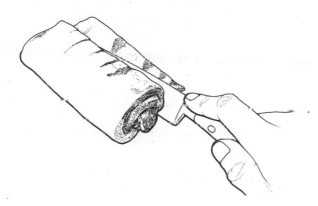

4   *Roll the meat up so that the nut of meat is covered with a single layer of fat and cut off any excess. Alternatively you can remove all the fat and wrap a thin strip of pork larding fat around the boned best end before tying and cutting it into noisettes.*

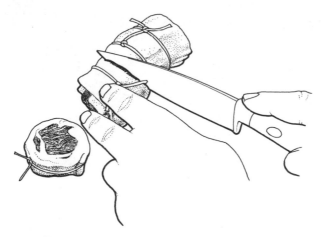

5   *Tie at 2–3 cm (1–1½ in) intervals, and if making noisettes then cut between each string. Otherwise the sausage-like best end can be treated as a roasting joint and very good it is too. The boned loin forms a superb cut for roasting particularly if it is filled with a good forcemeat.*

97

Preparing a crown roast

Use two or more best ends of lamb to make a crown and have them chined by the butcher; allow 2–3 cutlets per person with a few to spare. Three pre-packed best end roasting joints from a supermarket will produce a very economical crown, although generally you will have to do your own chining in this case.

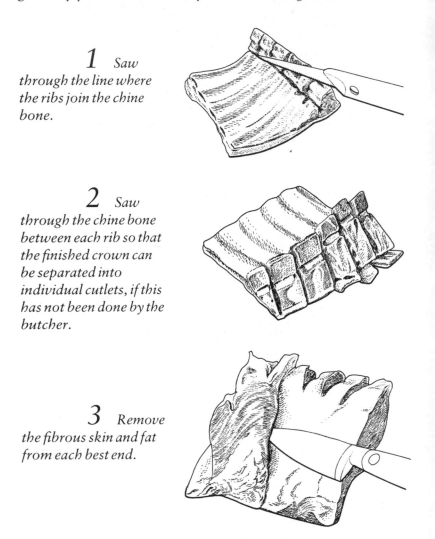

1 *Saw through the line where the ribs join the chine bone.*

2 *Saw through the chine bone between each rib so that the finished crown can be separated into individual cutlets, if this has not been done by the butcher.*

3 *Remove the fibrous skin and fat from each best end.*

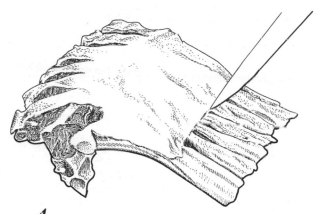

4   *Mark a line about 3 cm (1½ in) above the nut of meat and then scrape away all the fat and any meat adhering to the cutlet bones above this line.*

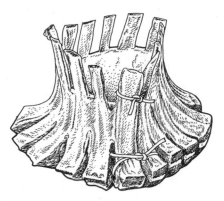

5   *Use a trussing needle to sew them together, with the fat on the inside and the curved bones on the outside. Note that there is one loop just above the line where the bones have been scraped clean and another loop through the angle of the chine bone. Wrap the tips of the bones with foil to prevent them from charring while cooking. Fill the centre with forcemeat, which will increase the required cooking time, or fill it after cooking with cooked new potatoes, a macedoine of seasonal vegetables or a sauté of mushrooms.*

Preparing a carré d'agneau

Get the butcher to chine a best end of lamb weighing a little over a kilo (2¼ lb) or do it yourself as described above in Preparing Noisettes.

1   Saw through the bones of the cutlets about 5 cm (2 in) from the fillet of meat running along the length of the joint, taking care not to cut through the fat or flesh of the cutlet.

2–3   Remove the chine bone and then, (opposite side) using a sharp knife with a rigid blade, cut out the short pieces of the bones.

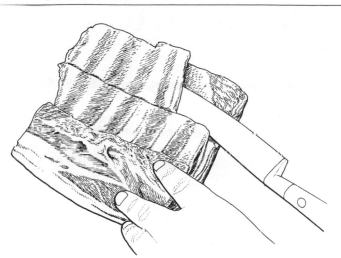

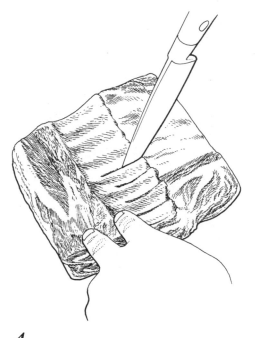

4 *Cut down one side of each cutlet bone and make a small slit across the end of each bone so that when you roll the fat and meat over them the bones will slip through easily.*

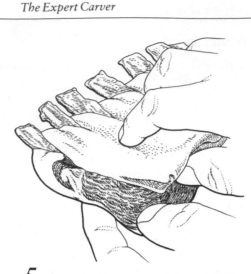

5   *Scrape the meat and fat away from each cutlet bone to within 1–2 cm (½–1 in) of the fillet of meat. Then press the flap of the remaining fat and meat around the fillet so that the bones poke through the slits and there is no space between it and the fillet. Cut off any excess if the flap overlaps the meat too much.*

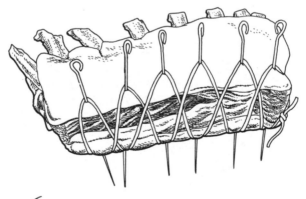

6   *Use small skewers to secure the joint and cross tie with string to prevent it from unrolling while it is cooking. Cover the tips of the bones with foil to prevent them burning. Remove the skewers and string before serving; the tips of the cutlets can be decorated with paper frills.*

General preparation of pork

You will find that the carving of any pork joint will be made very much easier, and the crackling will be first rate, if you follow the procedure below.

Make cuts through the rind and part way through the fat at roughly every centimetre ($\frac{1}{2}$ in) around the joint, across the grain of the meat. Take care that the cuts do not go through the meat itself as this will allow the juices to escape while it is cooking and the finished dish will not be succulent. If the rind is a little dry and difficult to cut cover it with a wet cloth and leave in a cool place for an hour or so for it to soften. Sprinkle the cloth with water if it dries out. When the joint is cooked you can use the lines in the crackling as a guide or pattern to the carving – a kind of 'cut me here'. See below which shows a hand and spring which has been prepared for braising. Note particularly how the lines follow the two masses on either side of the knuckle and the triangular strips at the base of the knuckle. They also indicate the basic plan of how to carve the joint.

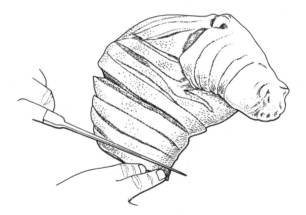

The various supermarket 'pork roast joints' often benefit from having two skewers inserted horizontally, at right angles to each other, and then being laced with extra string before being roasted, as they will then retain their shape.

Boning a loin of pork

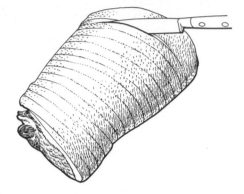

1   *I prepare the rind of the pork before I start boning it; you may prefer to leave this stage to last. Make a series of cuts, through the rind and about half way into the fat immediately below it, at a little less than 1 cm (½ in) apart. This allows some of the excess fat to melt away while it is cooking and ensures that the crackling is really crisp. Make sure that the cuts go from one edge of the rind to the other or you will have to break the crackling when you come to carve it.*

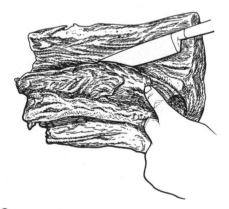

2   *Lay the loin on a cutting board so that the rind is on the underside and remove the fillet, disposing of any excess fat attached to it.*

3 Turn
*the joint around and cut
along the line of the
spine.*

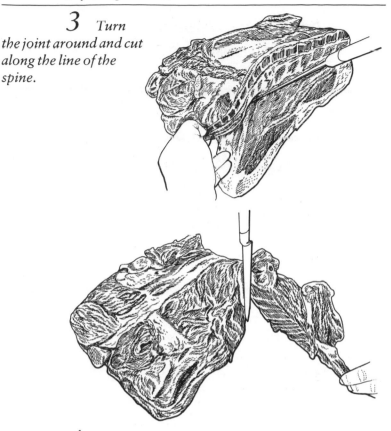

4 *Continue cutting along the loin bone and finally
remove completely. Cut away any excess fat from within the now
boneless loin.*

5 Fold the
*two leaves of the loin
over, replacing the fillet
in between them, and
secure them with
skewers, crosslacing the
skewers with string.
Turn the rolled loin the
other way up for cooking.*

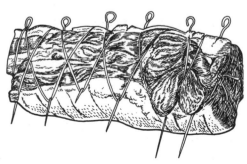

Barding and larding

Barding and larding keeps lean meat, fish, poultry and game moist while it cooks. If one is dealing with a fairly small bird, piece of meat or fish it is sufficient to wrap a thin layer of pork fat or bacon around it and, if necessary, secure it with string and a couple of skewers. This process is known as barding. In larding one actually threads lardons, thin strips of firm pork fat or bacon, through the meat; the process is not only efficient but the finished product is decorative.

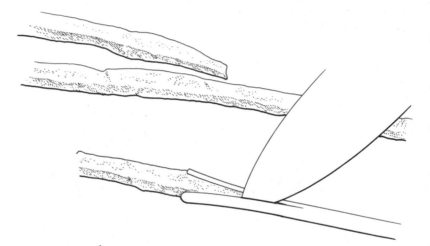

1 Chill the slab of fat, preferably from the back of the animal just below the skin of the loin, for a couple of hours before you start. Remove it from the refrigerator and, using a sharp straight-backed knife, cut it into slices and then the slices into strips. Load the larding needle with a strip of fat, pulling it into the wide end with the point of a small knife.

2 *Push the point of the needle through the meat, almost as if you were taking a tuck in it. Pull it through, releasing the lardon when there are equal tails on both side and then trim off any excess. Continue until the entire surface has been larded. Alternatively, the lardons can be pushed through the centre of the meat. This is particularly effective with cuts such as silverside or topside, or for that great dish from French bourgeois cooking, boeuf à la mode.*

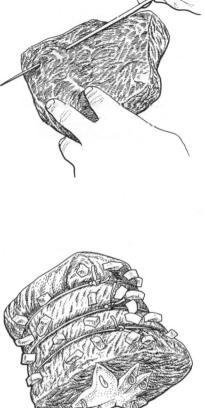

3 *A larded contrefilet; note the additional piece of larding, secured with small skewers at either end of the fillet to keep the ends of the meat moist.*

One can lard a large fish such as a carp, cod or sturgeon in a similar fashion. This procedure was used more frequently in the past than it is now. I was pleasantly surprised, however, with the improvement it made, when I first tried it, to an Indian recipe for braised cod; it kept the flesh deliciously moist and tender.

The thickness and spacing of the lardons control the quantity of fat that will be released to keep the food moist. A lardon of ½ cm (¼ in) inserted every 5 cm (2 in) is about average. A very pleasant variation is to marinate the lardons in wine and herbs before inserting them into the food. Put them in a bowl when they are all cut and pour over the marinade. Cover and return them to the refrigerator for another couple of hours before using them.

Barding a small chicken or game bird

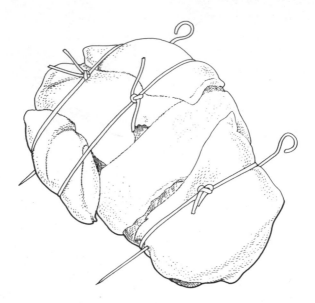

Cut thin sheets ½ cm (¼ in) thick from a block of larding fat; do not worry if they are not large as you can overlap them. Place a piece over the breast and then cover the legs with separate pieces. Overlap the pieces if they are too small to cover the breast completely.

Secure them with loops of string, using separate loops for the legs as the breast piece is removed towards the end of the cooking period to allow the breast to brown. You can also remove the pieces over the legs, but as they are inclined to dry out I prefer to leave them covered, although it does present a somewhat odd spectacle when you start carving it, as your bird will appear to be wearing pale stockings. Note the two skewers securing the legs and wings in position.

Marinating

Marinating meat, fish, poultry or game adds flavour to the finished dish, helps to make the flesh more tender and helps to prevent it from drying out during the cooking. It is simply a process of soaking the food in a well-flavoured mixture of wine, oil and herbs or yoghurt, lemon juice and spices for a couple of hours or longer. It should be an almost standard routine in all meat cooking.

In the following recipes mix all the ingredients for the relevant marinade together and place the meat or fish in a shallow dish just large enough to hold it, so that you do not require enormous quantities of marinade. Pour over the marinade, ensuring that it covers the contents and turn them over a couple of times so that all the surfaces are covered. Turn the contents over every half hour or so. Try adding aromatic vegetables such as carrots, celery, green and red peppers or fennel, finely chopped, for a change in flavour.

Red wine marinade
120 g (4 oz) onion, finely chopped
2 cloves garlic, finely chopped
$\frac{1}{4}$–$\frac{1}{2}$ teaspoon freshly ground black pepper
1 teaspoon fresh herbs, finely chopped
6 juniper berries, coarsely ground *or* 6 allspice berries, coarsely ground
280 ml ($\frac{1}{2}$ pint) red wine
150 ml ($\frac{1}{4}$ pint) olive oil

White wine marinade with lemon juice
120 g (4 oz) onion, finely chopped
2 cloves garlic, finely chopped
Juice and grated rind of a lemon
1 teaspoon fresh herbs, finely chopped (try fennel leaves with fish, tarragon with chicken)
$\frac{1}{4}$–$\frac{1}{2}$ teaspoon freshly ground black pepper
$\frac{1}{2}$–1 teaspoon coriander seeds, finely ground
280 ml ($\frac{1}{2}$ pint) white wine
150 ml ($\frac{1}{4}$ pint) olive oil

Eastern yoghurt marinade with cumin and lemon
120 g (4 oz) onion, finely chopped
2 cloves garlic, finely chopped
1 tablespoon fresh coriander leaves, finely chopped
$\frac{1}{2}$ teaspoon turmeric
$\frac{1}{2}$–1 teaspoon cumin seeds, finely ground
$\frac{1}{4}$ teaspoon ground cinammon
$\frac{1}{4}$–$\frac{1}{2}$ teaspoon freshly ground black pepper
$\frac{1}{4}$ teaspoon chilli powder (optional)
Juice and grated rind of a lemon
1 tablespoon wine vinegar
280 ml ($\frac{1}{2}$ pint) yoghurt
150 ml ($\frac{1}{4}$ pint) sunflower or groundnut oil

Preparing a tongue

The tongue should be trimmed neatly and formed into a round, with two skewers inserted horizontally through the centre, at right angles to each other. The roll should be further secured with loops of string tied around the circumference every 2 cm (1 in) or so; it is as well to use bows for tying off the loops as they have to be removed at the end of the cooking period to enable you to remove the skin of the tongue.

Boil it in a quantity of unsalted water, to which you have added a good collection of aromatic vegetables, for the time required for its weight. If the tongue is to be served hot, this initial cooking time should be cut by a quarter – see below.

Peel off the skin and remove any small pieces of cartilage or bone. Then form it into a roll again.

If it is to be served cold put into a pan of just sufficient size to contain it and pour in sufficient aspic to cover, leaving it under weights until completely cold.

If it is to be served hot, it should be reformed after being skinned, secured with string, glazed and braised.

Dressing, preparation and filleting of shellfish and fish

How to get the meat out of a crab

It is usual to buy crabs already cooked. They are at their best from May to September. Avoid any crab that is light for its size and any which have damaged shells; the first because it is an indication that it was either living on starvation rations before it was caught or that it had recently shed its shell, or that it was just out of condition. A damaged shell will have allowed the cooking liquor to get to the flesh which will, therefore, be watery. Also check that it has its full complement of legs and claws. Allow 225–300 g (8–10 oz) dressed crab per person.

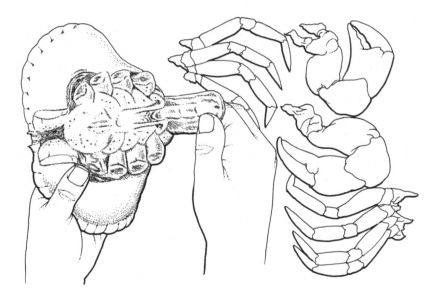

1   Lay the crab on its back and break off the claws and legs as close to the body as possible, by twisting them around. Leave them on one side for the moment. Similarly, twist off the bony tail flap and discard it.

2   *Using a short rigid knife, cut around the line between the shell and the plate to which the legs were attached, then prise it up, remove it and place on one side. Find and discard the small stomach bag and the bits and pieces attached to it, which will be close to where the claws were attached. Remove the spongy gills from either side of the bony structure and discard them. Use a teaspoon to scoop out the brown meat from the shell and put it on a plate.*

3   *Cut the bony structure in half and, using a skewer or fine-pointed knife, pick out all the flesh from the crevices, taking care not to get pieces of bone mixed with it.*

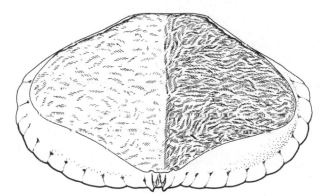

4 Crack the claws and legs with a light tap of a
hammer, taking care not to mash the contents, and peel away the
shell, allowing you to remove the meat. If you intend to serve the
crab in the shell enlarge the opening by breaking away the under
shell almost up to the boundary between the underside and the
top of the shell. Clean out the shell, making sure that there are no
small pieces of shell or cartilage remaining in the cavity. Arrange
the white meat on one side, using the larger pieces of white meat
from the claw for garnishing, and the brown on the other.

If you like, you can mix the brown meat with a few
breadcrumbs, a little cream, dry mustard, lemon juice and a dash
of cayenne. Dressing the crab yourself allows you to decide the
proportion of breadcrumbs and any flavouring you wish to add –
most commerical suppliers make it much too stodgy. It is
obviously essential if you intend using it in a recipe. While frozen
crab is obviously no substitute for fresh, it can be used when you
don't have the time to manhandle a number of fresh crabs to
obtain the required quantity. But use it only for ravioli or a
mousse where the texture and flavour of fresh crab is not so
essential to the success of the dish.

113

Dealing with a lobster

Unless you live close to the sea and can obtain really freshly caught lobsters it is probably better to buy them ready cooked from a reliable fishmonger. It is almost impossible to know how long your lobster has been kept in the fishmonger's tank with its pincers secured with rubber bands and, therefore, unable to feed. Always choose a lobster that has a good weight for its size and, as with crab, check that its shell is not damaged and that it has the full complement of claws and legs.

They are at their best from March to October; I do not consider that frozen lobster is worth buying as the firm textured flesh and that flavour which has so much of the very essence of sea food is destroyed and in its place there is a kind of watery stringiness and a very faint echo of the original flavour.

Allow 225–350 g (8–12 oz) cooked, undressed lobster per person, preferably a single lobster each, in which case go for the larger portion as a very small lobster is not a good buy. It is possible to split them in half, and many recipes suggest it, but I think it looks messy and mean.

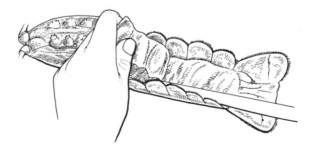

1 Lay the lobster on its back and remove the legs and claws by twisting them around. Put them on one side.

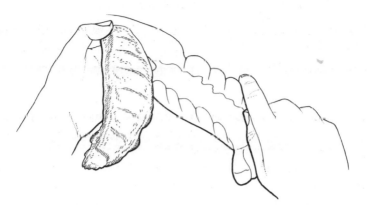

2   Cut along each side of the bony abdominal plate and then prise it up and discard it. Lift the flesh at the tail end and prise the entire strip from the cavity. Cut it into convenient sections for serving or eating.

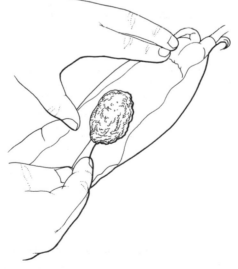

3   Scoop out the soft greenish grey liver and, if the lobster is a hen, any pink roe or coral. Discard the stomach sac which is at the same end from which you removed the claws.

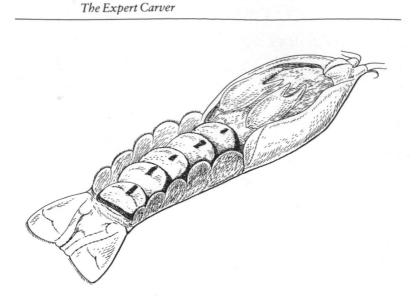

4   Crack the claws and the legs with a light tap from a hammer and remove the meat. If you are going to serve the lobster simply, arrange the liver and coral at one end and then fill the shell with the pieces which you have cut from the main abdominal portion and the flesh removed from the legs. Garnish it with the claw meat. You can reheat it by steaming for a short time but do not overdo it as it has already been cooked.

Opening and cleaning scallops

These are in season from October to March. Allow two medium-sized scallops per person or four small ones; take into account the richness of the flesh when calculating the exact portions. All molluscs live in sandy or muddy regions of the sea so particular care should be taken when cleaning them. Use a rigid short knife to scrape off any barnacles or hard deposits and then give each one a good scrubbing with a hard brush.

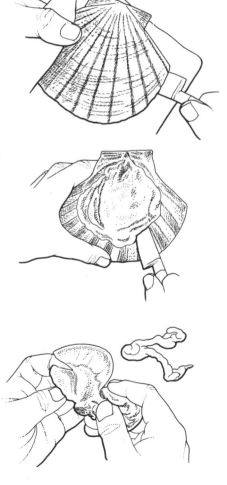

1 Hold the
*scallop with the curved shell
underneath, using a thick cloth
to protect your hands.
Manoeuvre the point of a rigid,
short knife into any suitable
cranny between the two shells
and then, keeping the blade of
the knife against the top shell,
cut along the surface to sever the
muscle that holds the two shells
together.*

2 Prise the two
*shells apart and slide the knife
under the scallop to free it from
the shell, taking care not to
damage the orange coral.*

3 Separate the
*white flesh and coral from the
digestive tract and the dark grey
stomach (which you discard).
Use the flesh and coral as your
recipe requires.*

117

Mussel management

Mussels are at their best from October to March, although they are now available all the year around. Allow about 350–450 g (12–16 oz) mussels per person. Discard any mussels that are not tightly closed or do not close immediately they are lightly tapped, because they are probably dead and, therefore, can cause poisoning. Also discard any that are unreasonably heavy for their size as they are most likely full of sand.

1 Rinse the mussels in several changes of water to free them from any surface sand and then, using a short, rigid knife scrape off any barnacles or deposits from the surface.

2 Cut off the 'beard', the filament structure protruding from the straight side of the shell and also scrape around the entire edge of each mussel. Finish off by scrubbing them with a hard brush.

Some authorities recommend that you now leave the mussels soaking, for a couple of hours, in sufficient cold, floury water to cover them so that they will become more succulent and disgorge any sand they might still contain. Use 60 g (2 oz) plain flour for every 1½ litres (3 pints) of water. Do not be alarmed if some of them open during this process as it is their normal state when covered with water. But it would be as well to discard any that do not close up when they are taken out of the water again.

118

Opening oysters

In Britain we subject oysters to the old rulings of being in season only when there is an R in the month, although they are eaten in Europe almost throughout the year. Specifying quantities is difficult – Colette is credited with saying that she did not like eating truffles unless she could eat too many; I am inclined to have the same attitude when it comes to oysters. I would suggest that a minimum number is six per person but a round dozen is better still.

1 Slide the oyster, flat side uppermost, between the folds of a thick cloth and anchor it with the palm of your hand. Have the hinged end facing you and insert the point of the oyster knife into the small hollow in the hinge. Push the knife about half way into the oyster and twist the blade to force the two shells apart.

2 Slide the blade along the underside of the top surface of the shell to cut through the muscle holding the two halves together, taking care not to spill any of the juice in the hollow, and then remove the upper shell and discard it.

3 Holding the lower shell firmly, cut under the oyster to release it from the shell, removing any pieces of shell that might have fallen in.

119

Filleting

Fish, to the anti-fish brigade and children, appear to sprout bones out of misplaced malice. The cook can assume the role of missionary by filleting the fish completely and thereby convert their guests to a more tolerant attitude, even turn them into confirmed ichthyophagists (fish eaters). Once the general anatomy of the different types of fish is understood the technique can be applied to any other fish.

Filleting a flat fish such as sole or plaice

The spine lies more or less in the centre between the two 'leaves' of fish like sole or plaice and therefore it is a simple matter to remove it. Some flat fish have a row of very fine bones on either side of the body and it is as well to remove this hazard before cooking them.

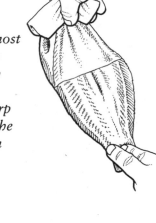

1 Lift the skin off the tail with the point of a knife. Then, using the tips of your fingers, loosen enough of the skin to be able to get a good grip of it.

2 Holding the fish firmly, grip the skin with a kitchen towel and pull it off. Keep the angle of the skin almost parallel to the board to lessen the chance of pulling the flesh away from the bone. If this starts to occur, use a very sharp knife to ease the flesh free of the skin. Repeat the operation on the other side.

120

3 If the fish has a row
of fine bones down either edge and
you intend to cook the fish without
filleting it completely, remove them
with a pair of scissors. If your
guests are likely to be particularly
worried by the sight of any bones at
all it might be as well to remove the
second row, on either side of the
fillet, if you are dealing with a sole,
although you will remove some of
the flesh as well.

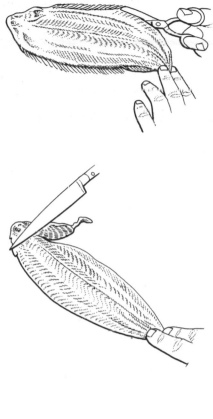

4 Remove the head
by making two angled cuts, one
through the abdominal cavity and
the other just behind the
'shoulders'.

5 To fillet the fish
completely make a cut down the
centre of the fish, following the line
of the spine from the head to the
tail. Then slide the knife under the
fillet and gently cut it free of the
spine keeping the blade of the knife
pointing toward the bone. Remove
the fillet and then deal with its twin.
Turn the fish over and remove the
remaining two. Use the bones and
skin to make fish stock.

(If you only partly lift the fillets
on either side of the spine, they
form a very convenient pocket for
forcemeat or any other garnish.)

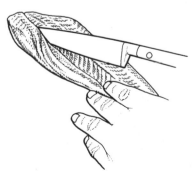

Removing the spine and rib cage from a round fish such as mackerel, trout, salmon or carp

The bone structure in a round fish is slightly more complex. However, if you follow the instructions below, keep your wits about you, use your eyes, a good, sharp knife, a pair of scissors and a pair of tweezers, you should have no difficulty. Remember to ask the fishmonger to clean the fish for you.

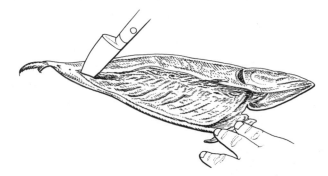

1   Wipe out the cavity of the fish and ensure that all the blood, vessels and the lining membrane have been removed. Then cut open the fish from the head to the tail.

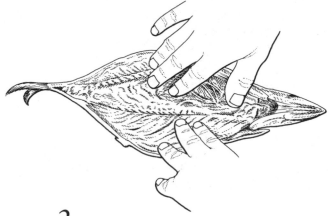

2   Lay the fish on its back and gently open the fish forcing the rib cage more or less flat, which will loosen the ribs.

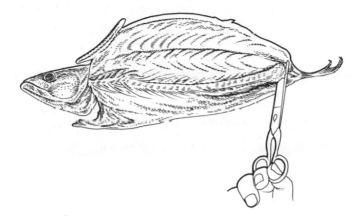

3   Slip the point of the knife between the sides of the rib cage and flesh and gently slide it along the whole of the cage – taking care, however, not to cut through the bones but only free them from the flesh.

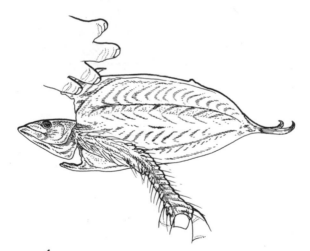

4   Use scissors to cut through the spine at the tail end and then gently ease it away from the fish scraping off any flesh that is attached to it and then cut it free at the head.

123

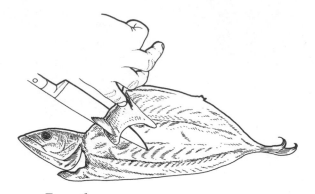

5–6 *Cut off the main fins and then remove the head. If you wish to serve the fish with its head attached you will have to compromise by only trimming the main fins as they will leave a gaping hole if removed. Remove any remaining bones with tweezers; slide your finger lightly over the fish to find them. Pay particular attention to the fin on the top of the fish. If it is large use a pair of scissors to trim it almost level with the skin on the outside and then remove the supporting bones from the inside. Close the body cavity by bringing the two sides together and securing them with skewers and crosslaced string.*

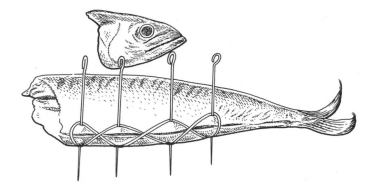

Index